# Creating Japanese Gardens

Created and designed by
the editorial staff of
ORTHO BOOKS

Editor
**Cedric Crocker**

Writer
**Alvin Horton**

Photographer
**Saxon Holt**

Illustrator
**Ron Hildebrand**

Designer
**Gary Hespenheide**

# Ortho Books

**Publisher**
Robert J. Dolezal

**Editorial Director**
Christine Robertson

**Production Director**
Ernie S. Tasaki

**Managing Editors**
Michael D. Smith
Sally W. Smith

**System Manager**
Katherine Parker

**National Sales Manager**
Charles H. Aydelotte

**Marketing Specialist**
Dennis M. Castle

**Operations Coordinator**
Georgiann Wright

**Circulation Manager**
Barbara F. Steadham

**Senior Technical Analyst**
J. A. Crozier, Jr., PhD.

**THE SOLARIS GROUP**
6001 Bollinger Canyon Road
San Ramon, CA 94583

# Acknowledgments

**Photo Editor**
Ann Leyhe

**Copy Chief**
Melinda Levine

**Copyeditors**
Frances Bowles
Andrea Y. Connolly

**Layout Editor**
Linda Bouchard

**Proofreader**
Leslie Cole

**Indexer**
Frances Bowles

**Editorial Assistants**
Karen K. Johnson
Tamara Mallory

**Art Director**
Craig Bergquist

**Production by**
Lezlly Freier

**Separations by**
Color Tech Corp.

**Lithographed by**
Webcrafters, Inc.

**Consultants**
Rod Baishiki, Belmont, Calif.
Shari Bashin, Magic Gardens, Berkeley, Calif.
Gordon Courtright, El Cerrito, Calif.
Jim Eggemeyer, landscape architect, Placerville, Calif.
Randolph Ford, landscape architect, Mill Valley, Calif.
Ron Herman, landscape architect, Berkeley, Calif.
Henry Matsutani, Matsutani and Associates, Inc., Concord, Calif.
John Nishizawa, John Nishizawa Co., Inc., Martinez, Calif.

**Photographers**
With the exception of the following, all photographs in this book are by Saxon Holt.
*Photographs are listed by page numbers and positions (T=top, B=bottom, L=left, R=right)*
Laurie Black: 95BR
Tom Bradley: 32BL
George Holton, Photo Researchers: 11TR
Noboru Komine, Photo Researchers: 7
Michael McKinley: 16BL
Susan Roth: 69TR
Tom Tracy: 8TR, 69BL
The garden pictured on page 69 (top right) was designed by and photographed courtesy of Mitsuko and Andrew Collver, Stony Brook, N.Y.

**Special Thanks to**
Marsha Atkinson, Gardenhouse, Burlingame, Calif.
Barbara Belloli, Fioridella, San Francisco, Calif.
The Bloedell Reserve, Seattle, Wash.
Daniel Campbell, University of California Botanical Garden, Berkeley, Calif.
Karen and Al Cooper
Tom Courtright, Orchard Nursery and Florist, Lafayette, Calif.
Emily M. Cummins
Lois M. DeDomenico
Professor Dolph Gotelli, University of California, Davis
Barbara Guarino
Richard Haag, Seattle, Wash.
Hakone Gardens, Saratoga, Calif.
Kay Hatsushi, K. Hatsushi Nursery, Inc., Pleasanton, Calif.
Mr. and Mrs. Richard L. Hawkins
Maz Imazumi, Berkeley, Calif.
Karen Jones, East Bay Nursery, Berkeley, Calif.
David Kato, San Mateo, Calif.
Kelly Park, Parks Department, San Jose, Calif.
Hoichi Kurisu, Kurisu International, Portland, Ore.
Mr. and Mrs. Allan Lee
Grace and Dan Lazorchick
Bob Lew, Berkeley, Calif.
Professor Gregory Lynn, University of California, Davis
Hiko Mitani, landscape architect, Rockville, Md.
Masa Mizuno, landscape architect, Lake Oswego, Ore.
Pat Morrison, Japanese Garden Society, Portland, Ore.
Bob Murase, Portland, Ore.
Shigeru Nakamura
Oregon Dental Association
San Mateo, Calif. Japanese Garden
Mr. and Mrs. Peter Stott
Strybing Arboretum, San Francisco, Calif.
Kevin Takei, Richmond, Calif.
Jack Tomlinson
Richard G. Turner, Jr.
Karl von Hacht, Berkeley, Calif.
Washington Park Arboretum and Japanese Garden, Seattle, Wash.
Mrs. James Williamson
Shirley Witt, San Francisco, Calif.
Betty Wood
Susan and Don Wrenn
Kiyoko S. Yamada, Berkeley, Calif.

**Front Cover**
This stunning yet simple garden (profiled in the final chapter of this book) blends many of the distinctive aspects of the Japanese garden: a rustic stone-slab bridge, a stone lantern and pagoda, the spring color of a Japanese maple, and a pond with koi.

**Back Cover**
Four scenes capture the beauty and tranquillity of Japanese-inspired gardens. Clockwise from top left: a stone lantern highlighted by flowering rhododendron; a rustic yet elegant bamboo water spout; a peaceful bench in the midst of a grove of flowering plum trees; and a water basin on a tea-garden path.

**Title Page**
This house is complemented by the dramatic Japanese garden. The bright Kurume hybrid azalea in the foreground provides seasonal contrast to the mostly green plantings, while the two large Japanese maples (*Acer palmatum*) lend a gentle shade to the patio.

# Creating Japanese Gardens

# The Japanese Garden: A Response To Nature

*More and more, Americans are looking to the Japanese garden for inspiration in their own garden making. It is not surprising that the Japanese garden—a tranquil sanctuary for contemplating nature—has a strong appeal in our modern world.*

This book is designed to help you conceive, plan, and construct a Japanese-style garden suited to your site and your own needs. You will be introduced to the spirit of the Japanese garden, then led through every process and technique for conceiving, planning, and building one of your own.

The first chapter discusses the uniquely Japanese concept of the garden's relation to nature, a concept that has influenced the Japanese garden through its centuries of development, and does, still, today. The five basic garden styles are described in a historical context. The essential background information supplied in this chapter will prepare you for the lessons of the book and for the challenge of adapting Japanese gardens to American needs.

Later chapters examine key design principles and components of the Japanese garden. Step-by-step instructions are presented for choosing and building the garden and for selecting and maintaining plants, including bonsai. Also included is an examination of a Japanese garden that is beautifully suited to its American context.

Throughout the book, the message of this opening chapter will be kept before you: The Japanese garden—or the American garden with Japanese spirit—is a living response to the natural world, which includes people themselves.

*Nature seems to have been touched just lightly by human hands in this garden. A Southern Indica azalea and a flowering plum provide brief seasonal color among black bamboo and evergreens.*

## NATURE AND THE JAPANESE GARDEN

In early Japanese history, the garden was no more than an area enclosed by stones, a straw rope, or a fence. The ground inside was sacred; the ground outside, profane. Over time, this garden has been elaborated on, diversified, and refined, but the original concept endures: The Japanese garden remains a place apart, where art and nature collaborate to create serenity. In the ancient Shinto religion, gods were nature spirits, so the Japanese people's perception of the garden as a place to worship nature is not surprising. Whether it is a postage-stamp-sized courtyard or balcony, or a spacious stroll garden, in every hour and season the Japanese garden offers the quietude of the natural world.

In Japan, a garden is neither a slice of raw nature enclosed by a wall, nor an artificial creation that forces natural materials into unnatural forms to celebrate human ingenuity. Instead, it is a work of art that celebrates nature by capturing its essence. By simplifying, implying, or sometimes symbolizing nature, even a tiny garden can convey the impression of the larger, natural world.

To what in nature does a Japanese garden respond? The answers are various. The garden is a response to space and form within nature: to the landscape itself, the sky above the landscape, the sea around it, and features within it, such as stones, plants, and streams. It is a response to natural time: to the shifts in light during the day, the cycle of seasons with their changing charms, and to the enduring aspects of nature. It is also a response to people, who, as creators and beholders, are themselves an essential component of nature.

### Response to Natural Space and Form

The landscape of Japan is striking, and Japanese gardens reflect its distinctiveness. The coastline, with its numerous islands, huge rock forms, and cliffs rising abruptly from the sea, is dramatically rugged. Wind shapes the trees, creating planes of sparse foliage on widely spaced, sturdy branches. The interior consists largely of steep mountain ranges cloaked with forests and streams and broken by valleys with fields, rivers, and rice paddies. Japanese garden design was, historically,

influenced by the picturesque landscapes of China, and some gardens still reflect that influence. Whether the inspiration is Japanese or foreign, a garden typically suggests a complete, coherent landscape and the subtlest forms, patterns, and unities within it. Successful Japanese gardens are created by practiced, keen observers of nature.

### Response to Time in Nature

A garden may respond to the passing of time in various ways. The progress of a day is reflected by skilled use of light so that, for example, in the early morning the sun illuminates a group of large, mossy rocks with their nimbus of rock fern. At midday the sun lights a seasonal accent of evergreen clematis flowering atop a fence or a snow-covered lantern nestled among low evergreens. In early afternoon the sun dapples an earthen wall or a mossy plain of pebbles with the cool, playing shadows of leaves or bare branches. In the late afternoon it backlights the perfect form and luminous foliage of an old maple.

The garden often responds to the seasons with short-lived effects that emphasize change and the passage of time. For instance, the intoxicating but brief display of Japanese apricot blossoms expresses the joy of earliest spring and the renewal of life. Water lilies

*Opposite: This late-autumn scene in the interior countryside of the island of Hokkaido, Japan, illustrates basic natural influences on Japanese garden design: rugged mountains, water, and forests of mixed deciduous trees and evergreen conifers. Below: A Japanese sense of enclosure is combined with elements typically found in American gardens: lawn and stepping stones. The back section of the house was modified to a traditional Japanese style. Azaleas and flowering dogwood provide spring color. The dominant evergreen tree is a deodar cedar.*

*Above left: Fallen petals of* Prunus serrulata *hint at the brevity of this dazzling spring display. The flowering ground cover is ajuga.*
*Above right: Winter reveals the delicate form of this flowering cherry and the subtle color of its small branches. The evergreen fern is a sword fern.*

float languidly on the pond in the heaviest heat of summer. A sprinkling of yellow Chinese redbud leaves on gravel marks the bittersweet melancholy of autumn. Bare coral stems of *Sango Kaku* Japanese maple gleam in the cold brilliance of winter sunlight and snow, emphasizing icy severity by providing a startling contrast to it.

The subdued, permanent garden features endure through the seasons and over the years, making more poignant the seasonal flashes of color. Rocks and other major landscape forms and the many evergreen plants, with their constant foliage, help to form the garden's backbone and affirm the continuity of life.

### Response to Man in Nature

The belief that people exist as a harmonious part of nature, not separate from it, and that in their daily lives they need to stay in touch with wild nature, is deeply rooted in the Japa-

nese character. Therefore, people have gardens. The proper role of people—in gardens and in nature—is that of participants, not of conquerors (as in a landscape reduced to geometric patterns—the gardens at Versailles, for example) and not of observers.

To remind visitors that people are a part of the natural order, carefully chosen artifacts are placed throughout the garden: a mossy lantern, a sunbleached water dipper, a worn stepping stone. Every artifact has a weathered, natural appearance that makes it fit gracefully into the garden.

To involve visitors in the fact that they are participants in the natural world, the garden stops short of replicating a landscape. It is left up to beholders to complete the picture in their imagination and to experience a simplified landscape as a natural one. When this happens, the garden has succeeded in involving the viewer most intimately—and has become the subject of meditation.

## DEVELOPMENT OF THE FIVE BASIC GARDEN STYLES

In this book the label "Japanese garden" conveniently covers all forms, or styles, as though they were one. Although they have some basic concepts and forms in common, each style is distinctive. Although the Japanese recognize a multitude of styles, it is sufficient—and most useful— for an American garden maker to focus on the five basic ones discussed below. Bear in mind, however, that the separation of "the Japanese garden" into five distinct styles is something of an artificial exercise. Many of the finest Japanese gardens and Japanese-influenced American gardens are mixtures of two or more basic styles. The garden that you plan and build may also be a blending of styles designed to suit your particular likes and needs.

Common to all the basic styles is a sense of space set apart from the everyday world for communion with nature. In various ways, every Japanese garden suggests the entire natural world. Each style recreates a paradise where time stands still.

Because each style developed and evolved in a historical context, enough of that context is included here to enhance your understanding and appreciation.

### Hill-and-Pond Style

Also known as the pond-and-island and the artificial-hill style, this general style encompasses a wide range of Japanese gardens. Older than the other styles, it originated in China. Like most of the styles, it was available in Japan, as it had been in China, only to the leisured, rich rulers, and nobles. The scale of a classic hill-and-pond garden is large, often immense. However, by observing some of the design principles such as simplification and forced diminishing perspective (see pages 28 and 35), you can create a successful version in a typical urban or suburban yard.

In China around and after 200 B.C., the founder of the Han dynasty and his successors built large gardens whose chief features were artificial lakes or ponds, symbolizing the sea, and hills in the ponds, representing islands. Emperor Wu built a garden in which the islands suggested the Mystic Isles of the Blest, then believed to exist somewhere off the coast of China. The isles, which, according to myth, originally floated, were believed to have been stabilized by the ruler of the universe, who ordered huge sea tortoises to bear them on their backs. But when a giant destroyed many of the tortoises, some islands floated away. The remaining ones, it was thought, could give

*This hill-and-pond style garden contains all the basic elements in a small area that suggests a much larger landscape. Lily-of-the-valley shrubs, Japanese maple, and vine maples provide contrasting colors and textures to the "hills" of the garden.*

immortality to whoever found and visited them (and Emperor Wu actually tried). In later Japanese gardens, small garden islands often took forms suggesting tortoises or, less often, the cranes that ferried the immortals to the islands. Both the pine-capped, tortoise-shaped islands and the less-representational crane island, which symbolize long life and good fortune, respectively, are still important features of many gardens.

One elaboration of the hill-and-pond style was the use of vertical rocks and waterfalls to suggest the spectacular Lu-Chan mountains in southern China, which were known to the Japanese through Chinese art. Monks and their disciples went to the Lu-Chan mountains to meditate on the natural splendor. In the hill-and-pond garden, mountains can be an alternative, and sometimes an addition, to islands. The garden became more and more a place for meditation, walled off but containing suggestions of the great natural world.

Hill-and-pond gardens, over their long history, have often incorporated whole ranges of mountains, represented by a series of earth mounds, or by low rock forms and low evergreens shaped to suggest the topography of Japan. Streams are often used instead of, or in addition to, ponds. In hill-and-pond gardens built since Zen Buddhists introduced the concept of the dry-landscape garden in the sixth century, cleverly constructed dry streams, ponds, and waterfalls are used to represent water features.

As with other Japanese garden styles, enduring evergreen plantings predominate over deciduous ones and green predominates over bright colors. Lanterns, trees, bridges, ponds, and other features are in exact proportion to the landscape. The scale of the garden landscape is usually smaller—sometimes remarkably smaller—than that of a comparable landscape in nature, but it is never so small that stepping stones, bridges, lanterns, and other functional elements are unusable or out of scale themselves. Ancient hill-and-pond gardens often covered many acres, but with careful use of the techniques described, even a small backyard can accommodate a hill-and-pond garden.

### The Dry-Landscape Style

*Karesansui*, the dry-landscape or flat-garden style, had precedents early in the evolution of Japanese gardens but came into its own as a major art form after the advent of Zen Buddhism in the late sixth century. It flourished in the small garden spaces of numerous Zen temples and monasteries, where monks used it as an aid to their contemplation of the essence of nature and human life. The dry-landscape garden is usually viewed from a slightly raised platform or a veranda and is not entered. In many of its forms, it is the most austere, sometimes the most abstract, and today clearly the most modern-looking of Japanese garden styles.

At one of its extremes, this garden is minimalist art, with so little form and detail that the effect is starkly and perhaps obscurely symbolic. Whole landscapes, even the entire natural world, are suggested through a simplification of form and reduction of scale. A

*Scotch moss, a skillfully pruned Japanese black pine, and an old stone lantern adorn this traditional Japanese turtle island. Carefully selected and positioned stones suggest clearly the head and flippers.*

typical dry-landscape garden is built in a small enclosed space that is flat or nearly flat. The sense of enclosure is strong—consisting usually of garden or house walls or a combination of the two. Plant use is minimal, and the few plants used are small and low, spreading or mounding rather than growing vertically. The spare features merely suggest mountains, valleys, plains, and streams or the sea. Water may be represented by an expanse of moss or other fine ground cover such as lawn grass. Typically, however, the dry-landscape garden is made of white sand, fine gravel, stone chips, or pebbles, carefully raked into stylized patterns suggesting the natural patterns of water. An edging of rocks and some plants is common. Simple, naturalistic bridges, such as flat slabs of uncut stone, suit this style. An evergreen backdrop beyond the walls is a standard feature in dry-landscape gardens. Sometimes the designer uses borrowed scenery—a view beyond the garden which appears to be a part of it.

The most celebrated example of this style displays the dry landscape at its most austere and abstract. In the garden at the Ryoan-ji monastery in Kyoto, there are no plants, except mosses on and around the rocks. An area of carefully raked white gravel measuring approximately 30 by 75 feet surrounds 15 stones

*Above: Entering the famous garden of sand and stones at Ryoan-ji monastery in Kyoto, Japan, you move into a space where natural forms are so abstracted and subtly arranged that the garden seems to encourage quiet, careful contemplation to be fully appreciated.*
*Left: Stones suggest islands and raked gravel represents water in this formally elegant, highly stylized version of the dry-landscape style. Dogwoods and a tanyosho pine frame the line of sight.*

*This dry landscape garden could almost have been created by nature—except that gravel replaces water. Less stylized than the formal, raked-gravel dry garden, gardens of this sort are intended to suggest natural settings.*

arranged in 5 groups. Beyond the wall, high trees, which did not exist when the garden was built, soften the overall effect. The garden, so startlingly non-representational of discernible landscape, is somehow essentially natural. The arrangement of its stones provides a complex example of asymmetrical balance, a concept defined in the next chapter (see page 37).

The other extreme of the dry landscape style, one which is relatively naturalistic, is a more recent development and uses the same materials as, and in many ways has much in common with the more abstract extreme. Seemingly natural water features characterize this style. Convincingly realistic streambeds, designed to look like actual, dried-up streambeds, are often used.

Streambeds are built to look so realistic that even viewers who know better might be persuaded that, when the rains come, the streams will flow again. Sometimes these dry

streambeds actually can provide drainage for garden runoff.

The dry-landscape style may be adapted to almost any flat garden area, though not in a great expanse; its features are designed to be contemplated at fairly close range from one point only. It is compatible, more than are the styles already discussed, with modern architecture and poses fewer practical problems of creation and maintenance. Because natural scale can be enormously reduced, it offers the ideal solution to garden making in a small space. It permits you to represent any natural water feature in your garden when an actual water feature is not feasible or desirable. A successful dry-landscape garden is also one of the most appealing landscapes to contemplate.

## Tea-Garden Style

A sixteenth-century outgrowth of the Zen influence on Japanese culture, the Japanese tea garden is participatory. It requires that the guest move over a path that leads, in a real as well as figurative sense, toward a fuller appreciation of natural harmony. This *roji*, or "dewy path" as it is popularly known, has great traditional significance in the tea-garden. Along the path the calmness and subtle beauty of the natural world soothe the spirit, remove worldly care, and prepare each guest for the tea ceremony. Meditative detachment from the world and rustic simplicity characterize this style.

The tea garden requires just enough space for a path through a narrow outer garden to an enclosed inner garden, which contains a waiting pavilion, or a bench and a teahouse, and a touch of rock and greenery. The basic layout, which is popular in the United States, lends itself to typical yards with their narrow sides and more spacious back areas that can be made private.

Features of the tea garden are few and simple, but must be chosen and arranged with great care. Form follows function perfectly; little about the tea garden is purely ornamental. Stepping stones, usually surrounded by moss, provide firm, dry footing and mark the path into the inner garden.

The size, surface, and arrangement of the stones can regulate the visitors' pace and heighten their awareness of what lies along the way. By slowing the pace, the path can

*Right: Stepping stones and a bamboo gate lead the visitor into the inner tea garden, toward the stone water basin, and on to the tea house (out of view here). Plantings, like the artifacts, are simple and restful. Below: This arrangement of basin, auxiliary stones, and lantern is traditional in a Japanese tea garden. Oregon grape, black bamboo, and Japanese lace fern are prominent in this simple planting.*

create the illusion of a larger space and a greater distance. A large, comfortable stone can be an invitation to pause and look closely at whatever is placed nearby. The route is softly lit in the evening by simple, weathered stone lanterns. The path is private; its simplicity and seclusion provide a mental and physical transition from the workaday world to the serenity of the teahouse. The mostly evergreen plants are appropriately restrained and unobtrusive, chosen to soothe rather than to excite or startle. Toward the end of the path is a stone water basin surrounded by gravel and perhaps some carefully arranged stones (see page 59). A stone lantern illuminates the water basin. In an authentic old Japanese tea garden, a nearby well would provide water for the basin and the teahouse.

You can adapt the Japanese tea-garden style, in both form and function, to an occidental setting and life-style. In a city or suburb, the tea garden can provide a place of calm for your own solitude and pleasure or for shared enjoyment with a few friends. As long as you provide privacy and an atmosphere of intimacy through the use of fences, walls, or dense evergreen screens and a roofed structure, you will achieve the spirit of the Japanese tea garden; copying every detail of the traditional version is unnecessary.

## Stroll Style

Similar in overall appearance, expansiveness, and detail to many hill-and-pond gardens, a stroll garden has, however, a basic functional difference: To be appreciated, it must be walked through and contemplated from many vantage points. Never does it reveal all or even most of itself from any one spot. It provides a quiet haven for meditation, but the viewer must participate more actively than in most gardens of other styles. Because it must be large enough for strolling, unlike the hill-and-pond garden, there is no possibility of reducing its scale to fit an area of only a few square feet. A stroll garden must be spacious enough to allow turns in the path and, usually, some changes in level. A garden of average to large size will provide sufficient area to accommodate a stroll garden if the space is well designed.

The idea of anticipating and then discovering beauty, detail by detail, is central to the stroll-style garden. Such beauty is often subtle, so its discovery requires a pleasant effort by the stroller. Together with the effect of the directing path, introduced in the Zen tea garden, the principle of hide-and-reveal, by which aspects of the garden are sequentially disclosed to the viewer, became prominent in stroll gardens as a means by which the viewer experienced their beauty.

The design of the stroll garden exercises considerable influence over the strollers. A dramatic example of hide-and-reveal is to be found in a garden villa built during Japan's feudal era. Every step along the path is ingeniously planned to control the strollers' experience of the garden. At one point along the path, the stepping stones become smaller, their surfaces uneven, and their spacing irregular, so that strollers are forced to look down, minding their step. Then the stones become smooth, large, and evenly spaced so that at an exactly planned point, strollers will raise their heads to see one of the most stunning vistas in any Japanese garden.

Paths that repeatedly shift direction by moving in a zigzag pattern rather than along a straight line, reveal unexpected vistas and provide fresh views of familiar features that a stroller might already have seen from other angles. In this way, the unique qualities of the stroll garden are revealed.

## Courtyard Style

Through most of Japanese history, the wealth and the ability to make gardens belonged only to the imperial family and the high ranks of nobility. Japanese society was sharply split between upper and lower classes. After the advent of Zen Buddhism, monks were allowed to make small, inexpensive gardens in and around the temples and monasteries, but it was not until the development of a prosperous middle class that gardens become possible for all levels of society. Because some commoners grew richer than their social superiors, it became necessary for them to disguise their affluence. The courtyard style was more private and had wider appeal than the tea garden.

For years before their wide popularity, courtyard gardens had been made at palaces, to be viewed from single rooms or apartments; at monasteries and temples, for peace and meditation; and as the inner portions of tea gardens. In even the humblest and most crowded urban areas, the courtyard style permitted households with a tiny patch of ground to enjoy the living, natural world.

The components of courtyard gardens have varied throughout their history. Following the invention of tea gardens, courtyard gardens incorporated three traditional basic tea-garden features: a stone lantern, stepping stones, and a stone water basin. These features, unlike their counterparts in tea gardens, are nearly always ornamental rather than functional, and the courtyard is never walked in. Most courtyard gardens use evergreen plants suited to such growing conditions as low light. Some courtyards use only a stone lantern, a few plants, and moss or gravel; others use plants and a basin; others use only a grouping of plants, such as a simple clump of bamboo. The stark garden at Ryoan-ji (see page 11) uses only rocks, gravel, and moss.

The Japanese consider one principle to be of paramount importance in making courtyard gardens: The components must be full-sized. Miniaturization would emphasize the smallness of the garden and destroy the illusion of the courtyard's being just one corner of a much larger garden that extends out of view. This illusion is important because a courtyard is usually open only to a patch of sky and can, therefore, feel more like the indoors than the outdoors. The illusion can be reinforced by use

*The path of this stroll garden leads walkers around a pond, where reflections enhance the beauty of plants and artifacts. Spring-blooming trees are at their peak of blossom; the weeping willow is nearly in full leaf; and at the pond's edge emerging Japanese iris foliage hints at later seasonal color.*

*This stroll garden in the Pacific Northwest displays asymmetrically balanced stones in a setting of moss with Douglas firs and other native trees. The carpet of moss has taken years to cover the ground perfectly. The disappearing path promises to reveal hidden beauties beyond the bend.*

*Right: This master bedroom has a private courtyard garden. Bamboo and a weeping form of blue atlas cedar dominate the simple planting. Shifting of sunlight and shadow create interesting patterns through the day, and movement of the bamboo in the breeze adds life.*

*Below: This courtyard garden uses gravel, old brick, and a lantern to create a simple and serene setting. Japanese maple, Japanese aucuba, and mondo grass temper the stone and provide changing color.*

of tall, pliant plants such as bamboo, which the least air movement will set into motion. Shadows of the moving plants play across garden surfaces, accentuating the presence of wind and adding to the feeling of the great outdoors. An effective courtyard garden might include the trunk of a tree whose top rises above the house, together with smaller plants and realistically scaled artifacts, to create an uncrowded artistic representation of the natural world.

In addition to natural scale, other principles are essential to making a courtyard garden look its best. Careful maintenance is essential because untidiness, in a closely observed small space, is obvious and unappealing. The absence of water can make the garden appear flat and dull. Frequent sprinkling of plants, artifacts, and gravel evokes the sweetness and freshness of the greater outdoors after a rain shower.

The courtyard style offers many possibilities to Americans. Postage-stamp patches of land next to a house or in an atrium can be used to recreate nature. If the garden is located in a small townhouse courtyard, a minuscule enclosed backyard. or even a balcony, the living space that looks onto it seems an extension of—and not sealed off from—the natural world.

## THE JAPANESE GARDEN AND AMERICAN NEEDS

Studying the development of gardening in Japan and grasping the underlying spirit of all Japanese gardens is an essential first step for Americans who want to create Japanese gardens. The most appealing residential Japanese gardens in the United States are usually living adaptations, not museum replicas, of gardens in Japan. You will be off to a promising start if you consider the Japanese design principles discussed in the next chapter and if you give some thought to a few basic observations made here.

### Adapting to the Environment

The Japanese have evolved several garden styles in response mainly to the natural world that surrounds them. Except for some fanciful imagery imported from China, the landscape suggested or depicted is Japanese. It is in the spirit of Japanese garden making for Americans to base their Japanese-style gardens on the natural environment of their own country. The American landscape is regionally so diverse and it is appropriate whenever and however possible to suggest the local landscape in the design of your garden. Explore the topography of your area for inspiration. Consider

*The beauty of the blue-oak woodland in the photograph above is enhanced, not violated, by the understated planting of Southern Indica azaleas and periwinkle shown in the photograph at left. The placed stone is harmonious with the natural-stone rocky outcrops in the area.*

using local stone rather than stone from elsewhere. In natural settings nearby, look closely at plants and the ways in which they appear, both individually and in groupings.

Also bear in mind the local soil and climate and their effect on plants. There are aesthetic and practical advantages to choosing plants, native or exotic, that not only are in keeping with Japanese spirit and aesthetics, but also flourish in the growing conditions where you live. To create and try to maintain a garden of plants not suited to your area can be expensive and unsuccessful. And it will not achieve the basic goal of the Japanese garden: to evoke the natural world.

Successful gardens in Japan are invariably suited to the architecture of the adjacent building or buildings. If the design of your house is very simple and modern, if glass erases the sharp division between indoors and outdoors, and if exterior materials are natural and mellow, you can easily have a garden with simple Japanese-style features. If your house has an older occidental style, you may want to rely on Japanese design ideas rather than on the actual artifacts and other features.

*The simple lines of the house and the glass wall unite home and garden effectively. Japanese maple shades the patio and provides an attractive foreground feature to be viewed from indoors or the patio, as well as creating overhead enclosure. Belgian Indica azaleas make a brief display, to be followed by rhododendrons.*

*The gravel-and-evergreen landscape, accented by a red form of Japanese maple, forms a welcoming street-side front garden. Notice how the simplicity of the design and the absence of Japanese artifacts allow the garden to harmonize with very non-Japanese architecture.*

*This hill-and-pond garden (which includes a small stroll path) displays colors at their heights. The garden might seem too busy if the color scheme were broader or if all color spots persisted the year around. Among the brightest touches are whorls of new pieris foliage and photinia. Douglas firs enclose the garden.*

Most styles of Japanese gardens lend themselves to limited spaces. Take advantage of this fact to make one or more gardens that unite your house and the natural world. Basic Japanese principles can enable you to make a simple garden, perhaps of a few container plants, rock, and sand or gravel, even on a tiny concrete terrace. But be careful not to crowd your small garden. In Japanese gardens, less is more. And avoid "cute" miniature artifacts that fail to stimulate the imagination.

## Adapting to an American Style of Living

Although life today in a Japanese city is as hectic and modern as in an American one, there are some basic differences that might be reflected in gardens there and here. Besides these differences, your own tastes and needs deserve consideration.

In both cultures, there is a need for privacy and for time and space for quiet and contemplation. Americans are more extroverted than the Japanese and often like to share their gardens, or parts of them, with the public. Most suburban American front yards are public space. At their best, they harmonize with the architecture, with other yards nearby, and with the surrounding natural world. At their worst, they clash with their surroundings, presenting a jumble of unrelated artifacts and overplanting. A successful melding of Japanese style and American needs may be seen in the streetside garden pictured on page 18.

In its American context, the garden offers a pleasing solution to the use of public space. In Japan, where a garden would never be so exposed, the outer part of a tea garden serves not only to lead guests to the teahouse but also to put them into a contemplative mood. Perhaps you would never use a tea garden as the Japanese do, but consider whether the narrow entryway along the side of your house might be made more inviting and calming by adopting something of the tea-garden style.

Americans often prefer color in their gardens. The extensive use of color often seen in American gardens has no place among the basic principles of Japanese garden making. The Japanese do use brief seasonal flashes of color in otherwise monochromatic gardens. As you proceed with your planning, consider how much and what kind of color will satisfy your tastes and, at the same time, meet the requirements of a Japanese garden. Look for the balance that is right for you and your garden.

A successful Japanese-influenced American garden may look authentically Japanese, or it may reveal its influence only on close and thoughtful inspection. Try to create a garden that, regardless of its style, provides sanctuary and a living link with the natural world.

# Designing Your Garden

*An appreciation of the spirit of the Japanese garden and an understanding of each of its traditional styles is an essential first step toward creating your own Japanese garden. Resist the impulse to create an instant garden.*

Three practical procedures are necessary for the successful building of any garden, regardless of whether all or part of an old garden is to be replaced or a new garden created. First, make a careful study of your own needs: What functions will your garden serve? Then, study the site closely: What assets and what constraints come with the territory? Finally—and here the focus narrows specifically to the planning of a Japanese garden—determine which principles of Japanese design will serve you best in the plan that you are developing. In this chapter several basic Japanese design principles are discussed and illustrated.

The first stage of planning, during which you examine your needs, can be especially enjoyable and productive—a game that encourages you to lay aside restraints and dream, freely and creatively. Whether you're setting out to design a small entryway garden, a spacious stroll garden, or various gardens around your property, you will profit from this exercise.

Keep a notebook of every idea that occurs to you, at every stage of planning. You may prefer a garden that is subtly or completely Japanese in style, but it is essential, at first, to stay open to all possibilities rather than to confine your thinking to one style. Include anything that shows, and can remind you later, what garden designs or features appeal to you.

*The well-planned structure of this new garden is evident when viewed from the raised deck. Seasonal accents are provided by Kurume azaleas. As plants assume their mature forms and dimensions, the garden will acquire a mellow, ageless quality.*

## EXAMINING YOUR NEEDS

Spend time at the garden site and see what inspirations and feelings it gives you. Here the process of determining needs may begin to merge productively with the next step, site analysis. Let the wishing-and-dreaming stage go on for days, weeks, or months—until you feel confident that you have covered all of your garden fantasies and wishes.

### The Substance: A Checklist

Consider each of the following areas and respond to the questions as specifically as possible. Then, consider each response and ask yourself questions about it. In the course of this examination, you will begin to analyze your site.

**Privacy and openness**   How you respond to these questions may depend on the location of the garden. Consider each question for each of your garden areas.

☐ How much, if any, of your garden do you want to be visible from outside your property?

☐ If you want public areas, what functions should they serve? Exactly what impressions should they make or effects should they have on people? What features can you imagine in your private areas?

☐ Are any of your needs at odds with the serene spirit of the Japanese garden that was described earlier? If so, how and to what extent? Which conflicts are easily resolvable, and how?

**Recreation**   Recreational use of the garden can mean different things to different people.

☐ What kinds of outdoor home recreation do you enjoy? What particular features, such as a lawn or a children's play area, does your ideal garden include?

☐ Which of these are high priority features and which are not? List each feature according to its importance.

☐ Try to imagine each feature in the context of your Japanese garden. Which recreational features will the garden accommodate and which will require a separate area?

**Repose**   You may want your garden to be, at least in part, a place of quiet and relaxation.

☐ To what extent does your ideal garden offer repose? What means of repose are most

*Above right: Two separate specimens of Japanese maple, planted close together and carefully shaped over the years, provide the graceful canopy for a patio dedicated to repose. Simple lines of modern outdoor furniture harmonize with the predominant Japanese feeling of the garden.*
*Below right: Unsightly plumbing and undistinguished windows are masked in a manner that actually enhances the beauty and Japanese flavor of this house and garden.*
*Below opposite: The recreational function of this swimming pool is augmented by its decorative value as a reflecting pool. The dark bottom is appropriate for any pool in a Japanese garden. The prominent tree is an atlas cedar. A mass of agapanthus provides a color accent. This garden was designed by Thomas Church.*
*Above opposite: A comfortable openness exists within the enclosure created by shrubs and medium to tall trees. The simple, angled bench of weathered wood affords the visitor a shaded vantage point for enjoying the garden.*

important to you? Again, list your priorities and distinguish between the essential and the optional.

☐ What kinds of structures, furnishings, equipment or other features does each important means of relaxation call for? (Remember, at this stage the sky's the limit.)

☐ Because repose is a frame of mind, visualize settings that would best accommodate each important means of repose. Write descriptions for each setting, detailing all features, structures, and any other elements conducive to relaxation.

**Entertaining**   Enjoying your garden in the company of friends may be an important element to consider in your planning.

☐ What kinds of entertaining will your ideal garden accommodate? Consider every possibility within your style of living, from sitting and chatting quietly with a few friends to serving (and perhaps cooking) dinner outdoors, to hosting a large cocktail party.

☐ Exactly what kinds of facilities and how much room does each type of entertaining require? Don't forget that you will need room for easy circulation and serving. Will you need lighting for evening entertaining?

☐ What arrangement of space and facilities allows large-scale entertaining without eliminating the possibility of intimate, small-scale entertaining or private use at other times? Do you need separate areas, even separate gardens, for large and small gatherings?

**Gardening and maintenance**   As important as these considerations are to most homeowners, they are not always given the close attention they demand.

☐ Who will build your garden and who will maintain it? Do you want a low-maintenance garden, or are you willing to sustain a higher level of maintenance?

☐ Aside from the tending of the Japanese-style ornamental garden, what other kinds of gardening are to be done? For example, does your dream garden contain a lath house, perhaps for bonsai that aren't currently on display in the garden proper? Which kinds of gardening does the main garden accommodate successfully and which require their own separate areas?

☐ Which of your favorite kinds of gardening create seasonal unsightliness? Can they be screened from view?

**Practical considerations**   Other important questions during the planning stages follow.

☐ What kinds of work must be done periodically to maintain your garden? What household services—such as garbage removal—require access through your garden space?

☐ What kinds of facilities, such as wide and solid pathways, electrical outlets, and hose bibs, do your practical needs demand?

☐ What kinds of work and storage areas must claim space that might otherwise be part of your garden—for example, areas for making compost, collecting refuse, housing heating and air conditioning pumps, storing garden tools, potting plants, or holding container plants that are out of bloom or season? Consider this last use of space carefully, because many Japanese gardens display container plants only during certain seasons.

## ANALYZING YOUR GARDEN SITE

There is usually no magic moment when the examination of needs ends and the analysis of the site begins. Site analysis is a close, methodical look at your property to determine its physical characteristics and horticultural potential, and a comparison between your needs list and what the property will actually allow. Whether you have an undeveloped site or an old garden, only careful analysis can reveal its potential and its limitations.

*A floor-to-ceiling glass door joins house and garden, encouraging easy circulation between the two. The awning and tree boughs provide shade and enclosure, while the paved patio and lawn beyond are ideal for relaxing or entertaining.*

## Checking Soil and Natural Elements

Having determined through your checklists what you would like from a garden, you are ready to begin matching your needs to the physical realities of your site.

At this stage it is important to work from a base map: a simple but accurate diagram of your property that includes its dimensions, the placement of the house on the property (with outer doors and windows indicated), and the placement of other buildings, driveways, and paved or constructed features. It is best to use architect's graph paper, imprinted with a ⅛-inch grid. If your garden area is large, let ⅛ inch represent 1 foot; otherwise, let ¼ inch represent 1 foot. If a map of your property already exists, it's almost certainly drawn to ⅛-inch or ¼-inch scale. You may need to use a tape measure, but if you work from the house plans, a deed map, or a contour map you can save hours or days of measuring and drawing, especially if you can trace the map. See sample base plan, page 27.

Unless your property is relatively flat, draw contour lines representing every 1-foot change in level, to show all topographic features and the exact gradient. You can use this information to map drainage patterns: rainwater and irrigation runoff routes, and spots where water collects. Bear in mind the practical or legal dangers of channeling your runoff toward your own house or onto neighbors' property.

Now study the natural elements and the soil on your property. The following list includes basic, essential information to be gathered. Record each item on your base map.

☐ Magnetic north. Draw an arrow on the map indicating where it is.

☐ Direction of prevailing wind.

☐ Windy spots. They're sometimes near corners of the house.

☐ Hot spots. These are the areas that get continuous sunlight.

☐ Cold spots. Because cold air flows downhill, like water, cold spots are usually in the lowest areas, or in areas where flowing air is blocked by walls or fences.

☐ Shady spots. Bear in mind how shady and sunny spots change with the seasons, with the angle of the sun, and with the leafing and shedding of deciduous trees.

☐ Soil type and condition. In some places the native soil is mostly of the same type—for example, all sand, or sandy loam, or clay. In other areas, or in isolated spots, there can be pockets or veins of heavy, rocky, or very alkaline soil.

### Checking Other Natural and Constructed Features

Continue your analysis by studying and noting anything on or within view of the site that might affect its use for a garden. Note and record each on your base map.

☐ Existing vegetation. Take note especially of mature trees and shrubs, and of such features as areas of bermudagrass or groves of bamboo. Label each.

☐ Natural topographic features. If your site has never been bulldozed and rock outcrops or other natural features remain, consider yourself blessed. They can be special assets in Japanese gardens.

☐ Unattractive views. These would include areas of your site visible from outside. Anything from an ugly nearby house to power poles and wires might affect your garden planning. Use arrows to indicate unsatisfactory viewpoints, and label each one.

☐ Attractive views. Not just panoramic views of breathtaking landscapes, but a tree or a mass of treetops beyond your property, or a splendid area in an adjoining garden, offer possibilities for enlarging the beauty and the scope of your garden. See pages 32 to 35, on borrowed scenery, for a discussion of the ways in which even very small or limited visual assets beyond your site can be "captured." Use arrows to indicate viewpoints, from the garden as well as from indoors, and label each.

☐ Essential site features. Include easements, setbacks, placement of meters, underground and overhead lines, hose bibs, outdoor electrical outlets, downspouts, and drainage systems. If you have not already noted fences and walls, do so, and indicate their heights. Indicate the height of each window or glass door above ground level.

Then make a list of your site's problems, in order of severity, and its assets, in order of value or attractiveness. Bearing in mind the spirit of the Japanese garden and remembering your own needs, consider solutions to the problems and uses for the assets.

## CHECKING NEEDS AGAINST SITE CHARACTERISTICS

Now the process becomes much more creative and stimulating than simply checking maps for sewer easements and noting elements in the scenery. A plan (or perhaps a range of plans) begins to emerge, as you compare what you want with what you have.

### Overlaying Sketches

At this point lay sheets of tracing paper over your base map. If the map with all of its site notations becomes cluttered, transfer some notes onto tracing sheets as well.

On the sheets of tracing paper, experiment with various plans for your site. These sketches represent your needs as they are influenced by the limitations and assets of your site. Draw circles (sometimes called "balloons") to represent areas and major features. As focal points or areas of the garden emerge, draw dotted arrows to indicate sight lines from viewpoint to object.

Draw large arrows to show circulation patterns. Decide how people will move from one point to another in the garden. Is the route logical and safe, and does it offer the best views of garden features? Include the paths of anyone who routinely or occasionally enters the site.

### Evolving a Plan

If your site already has a garden, give careful thought to what, if anything, you will retain. If the old garden still pleases you and its layout, contours, and atmosphere are suitable for a Japanese garden, you may decide to make only superficial changes. For instance, you may replace a straight brick path with a curving line of stepping stones, a flower bed with a stone arrangement and some evergreens, or cover a brick wall with woven bamboo or greenery.

You may, however, find nothing usable, not even the contouring. Consider carefully before you remove mature trees. Usually you can arrive at a plan that incorporates them.

When you have a basic plan that continues to please you as you review it over a period of time, you are ready to elaborate and refine the plan by applying appropriate principles of Japanese design.

**Base Plan With Notes**

**Balloon Sketch**

**Completed Garden Design**

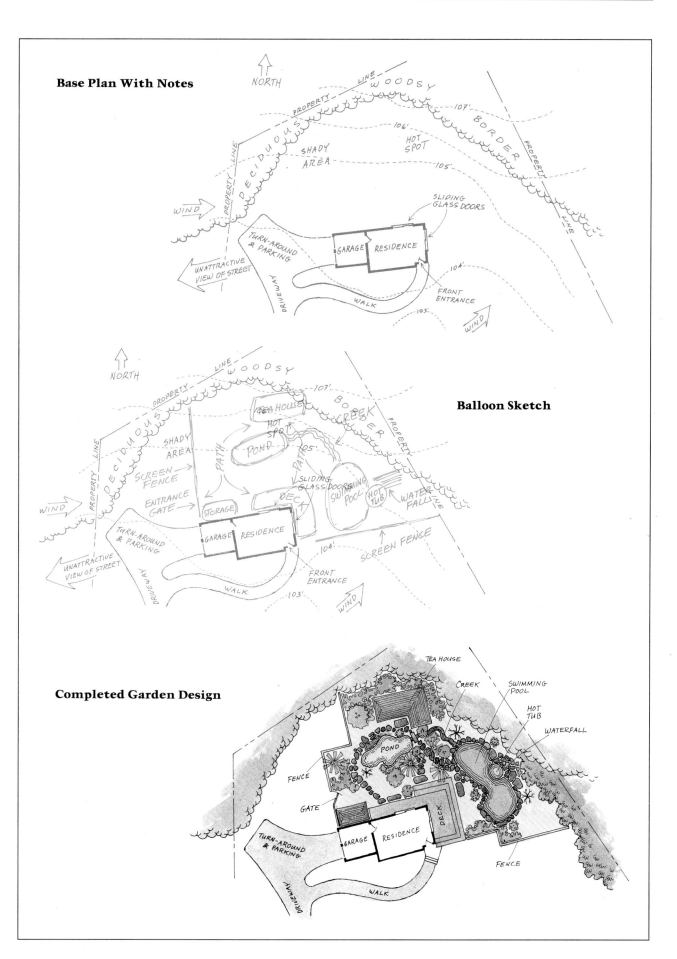

## USING JAPANESE DESIGN PRINCIPLES

It isn't a sprinkling of the trappings of Japanese gardens that makes a garden Japanese. True, the careful choice and use of garden components, together with both an appreciation for the spirit of a Japanese garden and a sound garden plan, are necessary to create a successful Japanese garden. But so are some basic design principles employed for centuries by the Japanese, and sometimes used in other garden styles as well. Discussed below are the key principles of the design of Japanese gardens, used just as artists use various graphic principles to compose paintings.

### Simplification

The principle of simplification, also known as reductivism or abstraction, is the reduction of nature, or some facet of it, to its essence. In garden design, this implies not necessarily reduction in size, but in complexity. The careful selection and arrangement of a few plants, a stream, and several stones might suggest the intricacies and conjure the spirit of a wood-

*Simplification effectively suggests a woodland waterfall setting. Rhododendrons and their brilliantly colored relative, pieris 'Flame of the Forest', together with two or three touches of other foliage, suggest a complete, natural planting. Skillfully positioned stones and an attractive constructed waterfall complete the picture.*

land setting. A few well-chosen stones set just so in a bed of raked gravel might produce the impression of a panorama of islands in the ocean. The smallest, simplest courtyard might successfully give the feeling of the most expansive of gardens.

The principle of simplification calls for active participation on the part of the viewer. Following this principle, a skilled garden maker closely attuned to the natural world can, with a few simple details, suggest a complex and perhaps expansive scene, and the sensitive viewer can then contemplate the suggested scene and fill in the missing elements. This phenomenon is rooted in every Eastern religion that recognizes, in any part of nature, intimations of the whole.

### Enclosure

Ever since the earliest Japanese gardens were enclosed to separate the sacred ground inside from the profane world outside, the principle of enclosure has been used to set apart the garden sanctuary from the larger world, and to unify the world within the garden. Without

*Right: In this gravel-covered courtyard, two specimens of Japanese maple, a clump of heavenly bamboo, and groupings of stones suggest an intricate landscape. In this instance the composition tends toward abstraction, encouraging the viewer's imagination. Below: From the indoors and from the raised veranda of this house— modeled on a traditional Japanese one—only the garden is visible. The eaves provide overhead enclosure.*

the enclosure or implied enclosure, it's very difficult or impossible for the garden or some aspect of it to suggest more than it literally is. Successful simplification occurs in self-contained settings, shielded from comparisons with the street or the surrounding open countryside. Japanese gardens have some overhead enclosure as well, and are bounded on one or more sides by the house. And the house is by no means an entity separate from the garden. Ideally it is an extension of the garden, and the garden an extension of the house, making a unified whole. Each may be appreciated from viewing points within the other.

**Outer enclosure**  Beginning on page 74, you will find a discussion of background greenery suitable for enclosing the garden and emphasizing focal points within it, or suggesting that the garden (particularly an extremely small one) extends further than it actually does. In very large gardens, masses of trees and constructed or natural hillsides sometimes serve to enclose—though in traditional Japanese gardens walls usually exist as well, even if they are concealed by topography or plants.

Walls and fences, instead of or in addition to living screens, are the usual means of enclosure in Japanese gardens. The styles, tones, and textures of such enclosures suggest age rather than bright, shiny newness. A weathered wood or bamboo fence, or a simple earthen wall, will not only provide a discreet enclosure, but will also unite the architecture with the garden.

**Overhead enclosure**   A primary purpose of Japanese gardens is to create a world apart, a sanctuary, a place removed from the everyday world. That purpose may be defeated if the garden is as open as a prairie to the sky. One function of trees in a Japanese (or any) garden is to provide a screen against the sky. A few trees, even one tree in a small garden, diffuse sunlight and create interesting shadows of varying depths. They suggest an enclosing canopy even as they frame sun, moon, stars, and clouds. The wide eaves that overhang a typical Japanese house provide a sense of enclosure that balances the openness of the sky. And balance, here as in other aspects of Japanese garden design, is most important. Never should trees or eaves obliterate the sky and create a closed atmosphere.

**The house as enclosure**   Typical Japanese houses, like typical occidental houses, have simple exteriors made up of regular, geometric shapes. A certain amount of symmetry is obvious. Their gardens, however, are composed of asymmetrical forms; natural, curving lines are most common. Yet houses and gardens harmonize.

How is this achieved? Typically a Japanese house provides its occupants and visitors some primary viewpoints into the garden, from both inside and just outside the house. Many courtyard gardens, for example, are created to be viewed only from within the house. Windows, or entire walls when opened up, remove barriers between the viewer and the garden. Corner posts and other permanent vertical supports frame the views. On some verandas, posts made from unsawed tree trunks suggest actual, living tree trunks, a desirable feature for the foreground. The scope of a view can often be regulated by sliding panels over windows. Floors of houses and verandas are usually raised a foot or so above ground level, affording open views of the garden, whether you are seated or standing. Even tiny courtyard gardens are designed to be seen from raised viewing areas.

Sleeve fences, extending from the house, provide effective transitions between building

*Above right: The view of this garden is framed by the eaves and the roof-supporting tree trunks. Rhododendrons and lily-of-the-valley shrubs in the background and a Belgian Indica azalea in the foreground show seasonal color. The red-leafed Japanese maple, here in early leaf, will provide subtle color for months.*

*Center right: This skillfully designed garden borrows the scenery of a forest that is not as distant as the constructed hills make it seem. The deceptively small Tanyosho pine and the fine-textured ground cover of the farther hills—bluish, in contrast with the bright green fore-ground, to suggest distance—trick the eye into perceiving a vast landscape.*

*Below right: Beyond the bridge and trees of the middle ground, the forested hillside provides a background of borrowed scenery.*

*Below opposite: A weathered fence encloses this young garden, and as they grow, the flowering cherry and Japanese maple will provide additional screening.*

*Above opposite: The superb old Japanese maple, shown here with its newly emerged foliage, creates overhead enclosure and a sense of intimacy within the water-basin area.*

*Right: What stunning vista or subtle detail around the bend of the path awaits the visitor? The deciduous Mollis azalea in the foreground obscures the view, increasing the mystery typically present in a hide-and-reveal landscape. Already in view is a fine mossy stone overhung by a weeping birch.*
*Below: This American variation on the traditional Japanese veranda has an added railing. The view is intended to be seen from standing level.*

and garden. Verandas, extending out over the inner edge of the garden, are also used as transitional devices. Stone- and gravel-filled drip troughs in the ground beneath the eaves combine the architectural lines of the house with the natural stone forms of the garden, just as, architecturally, the unsawed posts combine the indoor and outdoor forms. Other transitions may be made by placing container plants just inside the house, or by using split bamboo, rice paper, or some other translucent shades to catch the play of leaf and branch shadows and reflections from water.

Walls or fences that enclose the house and garden further unite both and set them apart from the outer world. Squared-off shrubs, along with rectilinear rocks close to the house and aligned with it, extending its shape, serve to integrate house and garden. Occasionally trees are shaped to echo the pitch and angle of the roof. Gentle slopes with arching eaves reflect the graceful boughs of pines in the garden. Frequently in Japanese gardens, living and architectural forms repeat each other.

## Borrowed Scenery

*Shakkei*, or, literally, "landscape which is captured alive," is landscape beyond the confines of a garden that has been incorporated into, rather than screened out of, the design. Although enclosure is an important principle,

the selective and skillful inclusion of outside landscape can enrich a garden immensely without compromising its sense of seclusion and intimacy. Enclosure isolates, sets a stage, creates a mood; borrowed scenery provides a balancing (and selective) connection with the world outside, drawing it into the design of the garden, even suggesting—in urban gardens, for example—that the garden is in the country. In every style of garden but the tea garden, borrowed scenery is appropriate.

What kind of scenery can be borrowed? Mountains, hills, waterfalls, trees (or just treetops), marshes, lakes, valleys, and the sea are among natural objects traditionally borrowed. Structures of special beauty, simplicity, and antiquity may also be used. Whatever is borrowed should complement the design and intended effects of the garden.

How are objects borrowed? Instead of offering broad unframed vistas, which can destroy all sense of enclosure, Japanese garden designers skillfully frame a borrowed scene. Openings such as windows or passageways in walls, gaps in dense hedges, or low-lying areas in built-up topography within or just beyond the garden have long been used. Traditional devices for framing borrowed scenery include high, branching trees in the foreground or middle ground, which serve to draw the scenery into the design of the garden; a gap or a *V* in dense groves of trees, designed to frame the desired scenery and screen out the unwanted; buildings, eaves, and veranda posts that may

*The picturesquely arching tree serves to frame the borrowed scenery in the distance.*

*Forced diminishing perspective makes this garden appear to be larger than it is. The small size of plants in the middle ground, near the miniature waterfall, contrasts with the larger foreground vegetation to give a sense of depth to the garden. Note the large-needled Japanese black pine in the foreground. Weeping cedar—representing a rocky mountain—and a dwarf Hinoki cypress are next to the waterfall. Scenery borrowed from surrounding gardens serves to further extend the perceived depth of the garden beyond its boundaries.*

**Forcing Perspective**

Pruned trees (fine-textured, small-needled *Chamaecyparis* and *Juniperus chinesis*) make the nearby waterfall seem larger

Mounding shrubs in middle ground

Large planter and Japanese-pruned *Pinus thunbergiana* in the foreground echo predominant lines of the borrowed scenery and, like the tree trunks, draw the scenery into the composition.

There is a technique, see page 15, of revealing to garden strollers a stunning vista at just the right moment, from precisely the right viewpoint. This technique is often considered a design principle in itself: hide-and-reveal. In stroll gardens, viewers following the paths laid for them participate in staged dramas whose object is to present borrowed scenery or features within the garden in the most effective manner. Such scenes or features may be revealed suddenly and dramatically— but the mysteries of the garden itself are revealed gradually, one at a time, rather than all at once and from only one viewpoint.

If your garden site offers material for borrowed scenery, make sure that whatever you borrow, and the way in which you present it, adds an attractive, harmonious dimension, enhances the feeling of apartness, and does not sacrifice the garden's privacy or sense of enclosure.

## Manipulation of Perspective and Sense of Scale

In designing a Japanese garden, you often will need to prescribe the viewer's sense of distance and scale. You might want to make a large area seem smaller, or, as is more likely, make a small area appear larger, for instance,

to trick the viewer into seeing a shallow area as being relatively deep. Similarly, one reason for using the principle of simplification (described earlier in this chapter) is to suggest a more expansive space than the entire garden, or a section of the garden, actually occupies. Manipulation of perspective is used create the illusion of depth and distance through practical, mechanistic means. Additional methods for altering perspective and scale are described on pages 74 and 75.

The phenomenon called forced diminishing perspective, used to give the visual impression of a larger space, is evoked in a garden when large trees, stones, or shrubs are placed in the foreground and small ones in the background. The effect may be created or enhanced by the use of bold textures in the foreground and fine textures in the background; by detail in the foreground and simplicity or lack of detail in the background; by the use of dark or vivid green in the foreground and gray-green or other soft, muted plant tones in the background, to suggest hazy distances. Similarly, if a path, streambed, or peninsula is tapered so that it narrows at the far end, and recedes from the viewing point, it will seem longer than it is.

The effect of forcing perspective is greatly enhanced by another perspective effect called obscuring the middle ground. In Japanese garden design, perspective is divided into three

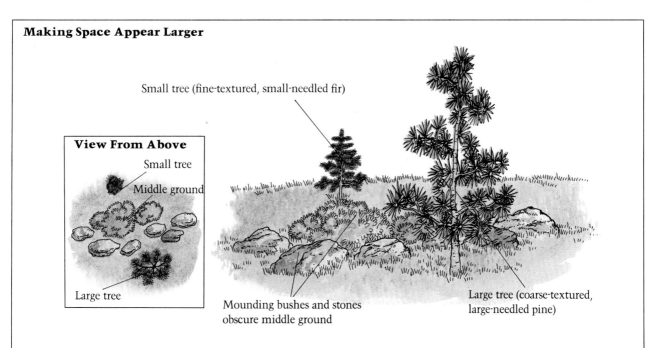

**Making Space Appear Larger**

Small tree (fine-textured, small-needled fir)

**View From Above**

Small tree

Middle ground

Large tree

Mounding bushes and stones obscure middle ground

Large tree (coarse-textured, large-needled pine)

planes: foreground, middle ground, and background. If the middle ground can be partially obscured by low, mounding rocks or plants, the continuous visual link between foreground and background is interrupted, making the background seem disconnected and distant.

A third method of forming perspective and the sense of scale is miniaturization. For example, imagine that near the bank of a pond in a garden lies a partially submerged boat, apparently full-sized. Because nothing nearby gives a sense of scale, this miniature boat does not give the impression of being small, and its presence makes the entire garden scene seem more spacious than it is.

Be careful in using miniaturization: dwarfed artifacts and structures can look out of place, partly because they call attention to the smallness of the area and the unsuccessful attempt to disguise that smallness.

To make an area seem shallower or smaller, all of the techniques mentioned above used in reverse will bring the background visually closer to the foreground. If you have a garden site whose depth diminishes the sense of enclosure and intimacy you desire, use larger forms, bolder colors and textures, and more details in the background, and make sure that the middle ground is not obscured. Taper pathways and other linear features so that their narrower ends are closer to the viewer.

*Above: Background shrubs and trees are actually quite close to the foreground, but mounds break the visual connection between foreground and background, creating a sense of distance.*
*Below: Clever use of miniature shrubs and trees and a small bridge create the illusion of depth. The scale of the patio furniture reveals the extent of the illusion.*

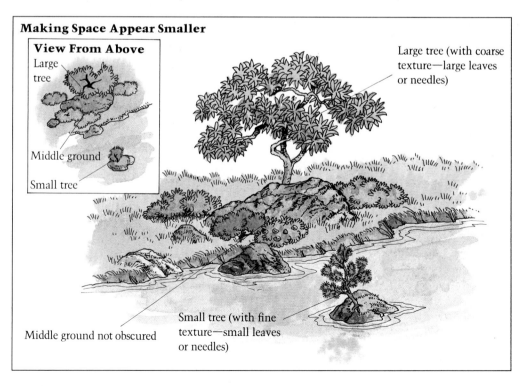

**Making Space Appear Smaller**

**View From Above**

Large tree

Middle ground

Small tree

Large tree (with coarse texture—large leaves or needles)

Small tree (with fine texture—small leaves or needles)

Middle ground not obscured

**Asymmetrical Balance: Interlocking Scalene Triangles**

## Asymmetrical Balance

The Japanese achieve visual balance in garden design through the use of asymmetrical balance (also called occult balance). Bilateral symmetry, in which the various elements are balanced in even-numbered groups of equivalent size (historically the hallmark of most formal western design) is alien to the Japanese. To make each side of a garden or feature mirror the other is unthinkable. The Japanese use the subtler, more natural asymmetrical balance in stone placement, stroll-path layout, and arrangement of most other garden features and overall garden design.

A seesaw holding two people of identical weight will be symmetrically balanced if both are at equal distances from the fulcrum in the center. Two people of different weights can also balance the plank, if the lighter sits further away from the fulcrum than the heavier. The difference in distance of the two people from the fulcrum will balance the plank asymmetrically.

In design, visual (not actual) weight must be balanced. A large stone has greater visual weight than a small one, even if the larger is a sponge rock weighing 30 pounds and the smaller a lump of granite weighing 70 pounds.

Psychological impact also influences visual weight. A gilded statue has more psychological weight than a shrub or stone of equal mass standing in the same position. A cluster of red flowers has more visual weight than a cluster of green leaves.

**Asymmetrical Balance: Single Scalene Triangle**

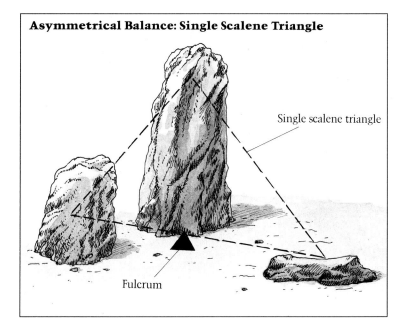

Single scalene triangle

Fulcrum

In a Japanese garden asymmetrically balanced designs usually follow the lines of a scalene triangle, each side of which is a different length. For instance, in a group of stones the central—and tallest—stone (or the vertical line that marks its center) represents the fulcrum, or balance point, and is flanked by two other stones of unequal sizes, to form a scalene triangle. Smaller "helping stones" (or mounding, dense plants visually used in a similar way) may be added to enrich and extend the group, but the asymmetrical balance is maintained.

Interlocking scalene triangles (that is, a series of connected scalene triangles) may be

*During the week or so of blossoming, the bright Kurume azalea has greater visual weight than the slightly larger lantern. When the azalea reverts to green, it will seem much smaller.*

used to develop more extensive groupings. As groupings are three-dimensional, not flat, the different elements are never lined up on a single plane but, instead, are staggered so that they lie at varying distances from the viewer. If the grouping will be seen from more than one viewpoint, the designer is challenged to make an arrangement that is balanced from every angle or, at least, from several angles. Japanese garden design also takes into account the relationship between form and emptiness, an important aspect of asymmetrical balance. The open sky must not rob the garden of intimacy, nor should trees, roofs, and eaves make too complete an enclosure. Open ground should be counter balanced with groups of plants, rocks, and other features.

## Unity

Like balance, unity is central to the spirit of Japanese garden design. The garden must encourage its viewer to feel at one, not at odds, with the natural world.

Ideally, architectural form of the house and the apparently natural garden blend together. The dividing line between the two is softened by transitional devices and by harmony of form. Garden and house are further unified in sharing an enclosure that sets them apart from the world outside.

Thoughtful choice and use of plants unifies the design of the garden and contributes to its feeling of unity with the greater natural world beyond the gates. On page 74 there is a discussion of the plants appropriate to the site and to the quiet spirit of a Japanese garden. Their use suggests, through simplification, the inherent unity of their natural environment.

Repetition will also give a sense of unity to a garden. A few plant species and combinations of species repeated throughout much of a garden, or in only one area of the garden, tie it together. The form of a mound may echo the form of a distant mountain. A low area in the garden or a background hedge may mirror the mountain's form. Angles, shapes, and patterns repeated throughout the garden unify it.

Stone is usually the greatest single physical unifier of the garden. Stones, in the overall patterns that they form, constitute the backbone of the garden. (See page 56 for a discussion of stone and its uses.)

Water unifies, whether it flows through or covers a large area, or merely stands in a modest basin and captures the sky. Paths form lines that tie the garden together and invite the viewer to walk through and explore it.

Surprises and discoveries themselves create unity. Particularly in a stroll garden, interesting bends in a path, a hidden depression beyond a rise, a shadowy glade, the arm of a pond that disappears among rocks and trees all lead the viewer onward and sustain a pattern of curiosity and discovery. Even in the most modest courtyard garden, the suggestion of a larger garden just out of view implies subtleties to be explored. The garden thereby has an appeal far greater than the sum of its individual parts.

Unity is also conveyed by complementary forms and qualities: the vertical and the horizontal, the bright and the shaded, the widening and the narrowing, the empty and the filled, the ephemeral and the enduring, the soft and the hard.

*Left: Complementary forms, the vertical and the horizontal stones, and the qualities—hardness of the stones, softness of the mondo grass— suggest wholeness (the ancient Asian concept of yin and yang).*
*Below left: Simplicity and unity are achieved by using only three major plantings in this garden.*
*Below right: The stream is the unifying element running through this scene. Also contributing to the feeling of coherency is the repetition of species, particularly the fern and the ground cover.*

# Garden Components

*In a Japanese garden, earth provides the matrix for the basic garden elements: stone, water, and plants. These natural elements, in various forms and combinations, make the garden.*

Stone, with its endlessly variable forms, serves as a building material, as a symbol for mountains and islands, and as stone itself, to give the garden its most enduring element.

Water, too, the Japanese find fascinating. To them it means purity. In one form or another, actual or suggested, water is the heart of every Japanese garden. Deciduous plants provide the Japanese garden with the transitory elements of seasonality, and evergreen plants maintain the presence of life through the entire year.

Stone and water, in many manifestations and combinations, are the principle garden components discussed in this chapter. Each element is considered on two levels: The concept behind the element and its relation to the garden as a whole. Then the actual nuts-and-bolts installation or construction is discussed. Construction methods vary enormously, so an effort has been made to present methods best suited to gardeners in the United States. Specific guidance in using stone, as natural form or as building material, is given. Water features that are appropriate for residential-scale gardens are treated in depth. Ways of enclosing the garden and areas within it, and ways of allowing and directing circulation of people within it, receive close attention.

Choice and use of garden accents, those touches that evoke a tradition and a spirit, are also included. Always, the spirit of the Japanese garden and the needs and resources of American homeowners have been taken into account.

---

*A plain yard is transformed into a serene world through the skillful choice and placement of stones in the landscape; construction of the stream and pond, complete with koi; and appropriate plant selections.*

# WATER IN THE GARDEN

It is not surprising that in an island country with abundant rainfall, water figures prominently in gardens. A simple stone water basin can capture the magic of water as surely as a waterfall with stream and pond can, and much more simply. A dry-water feature makes the viewer feel the living presence of water that does not actually exist in the garden.

## Waterfalls

A waterfall is nearly always the focal point of its garden, and no wonder: It marks a dramatic shift in topography. Usually it feeds a widening stream or pond that from downstream viewing points leads the eye to the waterfall itself, always in motion. Soothing water sounds cancel out noises beyond the garden and enhance the illusion of remoteness. You can emulate the particular charm of the natural waterfall by varying the seasonal volume of water, thereby reinforcing the mood of the season.

**Designing a waterfall** Most falls built in the classical Japanese manner consist of

*The small waterfall and pond with koi create a surprisingly natural setting in a narrow urban backyard. A dark sealer on the stones of the waterfall and pond enhances the calm, natural quality of the garden.*

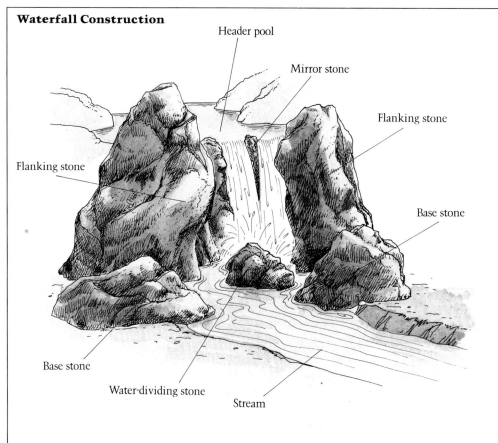

**Waterfall Construction**

Header pool

Mirror stone

Flanking stone

Flanking stone

Base stone

Flanking stone

Base stone

Water-dividing stone

Stream

seven basic stones, along with any number of other stones used to enhance or extend the composition. There are many possible variations, including simplifications on the basic configuration.

The mirror stone, the central stone of a fall, in front of or down which the water flows, helps to determine the style of the fall. The configuration of its lip—straight and smooth, or jagged, for example—does much to determine the pattern of falling water. In some falls an arrangement of stones, rather than a single stone, functions as the mirror stone. The position of the mirror stone also affects the way the water falls. If the stone leans slightly outward, water spouts from its lip; if it leans inward, water flows down the stone, unless altered by volume and velocity. The mirror stone usually stands no more than three feet above the water level of the basin beneath the fall.

At either side of the mirror stone, standing up to a foot higher and somewhat forward of it, are the vertical, more massive flanking stones. Usually these stones lean inward, toward the cascading water.

At the foot of each flanking stone, a base stone provides stability to the grouping by visually anchoring the vertical mass. Typically, base stones stand a few inches forward of the flanking stones in the basin beneath the fall. None of the pairs should match closely enough to be symmetrical.

Also in the basin, at its center, is the water-dividing stone that deflects the flow of fallen water bubbling up from the basin. Against this stone the fall makes its sound. Typically this stone is roughly triangular in shape and points upward into the fall.

A knowledge of the basics of Japanese waterfall composition may enable you to design a fall that delights you. But do not hesitate to call in a qualified professional designer to check, refine, or complete your design. After all, it's usual for a Japanese garden maker to serve for several years as a master's apprentice before designing a fall. Always keep in mind the appearance, sound, and overall effect you would like to achieve.

**Constructing a waterfall** A built-up corner of the garden can offer the perfect site for a waterfall, suggesting as it does an unseen

stream or other water source. You might consider using a sturdy garden boundary wall at the corner of your garden to suggest, from inside, a landscape that continues upward and outward. Wherever you position the waterfall, allow space for a small reservoir at the top, behind the mirror stone, from which water flows out in a narrow channel or a broad sheet to the lip of the mirror stone. Otherwise, water flowing directly from the hidden pipe from the recirculating pump will gush across the top of the mirror stone and outward, rather than spread and drop in the style you intend. Construction of the base of all but the smallest waterfalls requires the lifting and precise placement of heavy stones. Call in a qualified contractor unless you're confident that you can handle the work easily and safely.

Stones shifting and settling will crack mortar and cause leaks that can result in an empty pond and a burned-out recirculating pump. Be sure that each large stone in your waterfall is set deeply and firmly—and, if necessary, mortared to a steel-reinforced concrete pan. For most residential-scale waterfalls, however, such pans are unnecessary.

*This garden stream falls in two stages amid a lush mixture of woodland plants and mossy stones.*

Wherever water moves or stands in a waterfall, a liquid waterproofing sealer is needed to prevent leaks. Sealers are discussed on page 45, "Constructing a Stream" and page 47, "Constructing a Pond." From the small reservoir above the fall that feeds it, over all the mortared joints where the water might be lost in the fall itself, in the basin at the foot of the fall, and wherever water splashes in any volume against joints in stones, use mortar coated thoroughly with sealer.

## Streams

Even when they link a waterfall or simulated spring with a pond rather than function by themselves in the garden, streams have a particular vitality. In their connection to the rest of the surrounding landscape—topography, plantings, stones, bridges—they unify the garden and recreate in it a basic, lively natural landscape feature. In a spacious garden, even one without a waterfall or pond, the effect of a meadow crossed by a broad, shallow stream can be pleasing and natural. More often in a residential garden, however, a narrow and more winding stream may harmonize with a landscape that includes representations of hills or mountains.

**Designing a stream**  The basic considerations in laying out a stream are the scale of the garden and of any other connected water features, the nature of the topography, and the volume of water. A natural stream, rare in American gardens, is a boon to the garden maker (but also a potential problem, because of periodic flooding). Nearly always the water source will be a domestic water system. The volume of flow will be determined by the efficiency and power of a recirculating pump system. A given volume of water may rush or drift, depending upon slope and stream width. Depending on how it has been laid out, a stream of a given volume may have both rapids and quiet pools.

As do other aspects of a Japanese garden, streams with turns and irregularities corresponding to the topography suggest nature more convincingly than would a canal that functions like a sluice. A natural progression, especially if the stream originates at a waterfall that suggests mountainous terrain, is generally from a narrow channel with rapids

to a broader, smoother, channel and maybe a pond. In a short stream, such a progression may not be possible.

As you begin your design, consider the following aspects of the behavior of a stream. Water flows faster in a narrow channel, slower in a broad one. Slope affects the velocity of water. A slope of 3 percent is required. A greater slope is usually desirable.

Stones may be used to create an apparently natural partial dam and rapids. Fast-flowing water makes more dramatic rapids than does water flowing slowly. Just below a series of rapids, a stone dividing the flow helps to create white water.

At a turn in a stream, flowing water erodes the bank and the bottom of the outside curve. A turning stone placed in the water at the

*Naturalized mosses, fir trees, and lichen and moss covered stones make this garden stream appear natural. Note the weathered sozu (deer scare) at the upper end of the stream.*

## Stream Construction

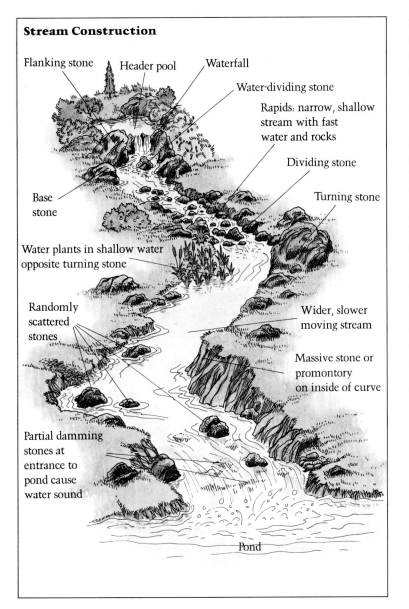

Flanking stone

Header pool

Waterfall

Water-dividing stone

Rapids: narrow, shallow stream with fast water and rocks

Dividing stone

Base stone

Turning stone

Water plants in shallow water opposite turning stone

Randomly scattered stones

Wider, slower moving stream

Massive stone or promontory on inside of curve

Partial damming stones at entrance to pond cause water sound

Pond

interruption in the surface of a streambed makes eddies, unless the water moves very slowly. A random scattering of stones in a stream looks natural. Too many stones lessen the dramatic presence of water, especially when the stream is viewed from any distance.

**Constructing a stream**    Watertightness is essential to successful stream construction. Beginning at the source of the stream (the basin at the bottom of the waterfall, or the simulated spring, if there is no waterfall), make a watertight paved bottom. Dig and construct the streambed so that its depth, except in pools, will be between 3 and 6 inches, depending on the available volume of water.

Protection against leaks can be doubly assured if the stream bottom consists of both vinyl sheeting and a veneer of sealed mortar. This stream construction technique, identical to that for the vinyl pond bottom described on page 47, will support stones weighing up to about 200 pounds.

The streambed may be disguised or concealed in a variety of ways. Over the sides you can trowel about an inch of soft mortar, one small area at a time, and push pebbles into the mortar in random patterns. After an hour or so, use a paintbrush and water to smooth the mortar between the pebbles, making it less visible and more tightly binding. You can enhance the natural appearance of the streambed by spreading at least two grades of gravel (neither of them smaller than ½-inch size) and some cobbles over the paved surface. Pebbles, gravel, and cobbles can easily be removed in the event that the paved bottom needs to be repaired.

## Ponds

The most imposing feature of a stroll or a hill-and-pond garden is usually the pond. Nestling low in the landscape, the pond anchors the garden and its surface mirrors the sky and catches the wind. The rest of the garden is designed around it. The openness of a well-designed pond strikes a balance with trees, stones, structures, and landforms. The concavity of the pond creates a balancing convexity: Soil from the excavation may become a mound in the garden.

If a tiny garden can't accommodate a pond, a water basin or a small pool can still reflect

outer bank will protect the stream bank and bottom. Even if the streambed is concrete, the turning stone adds a look of natural stability and smooths the flow of water around the curve. On the shallow shore opposite, some vegetation—perhaps an appropriate grasslike water plant at the water's edge—creates a satisfying balance. A massive stone, a mound, or a promontory on the inside of a curve lends an apparently natural justification to the curve, although the inside of every curve need not be treated in this way. Stream borders will look unobtrusive and effective if the rocks and vegetation are not matched and lined up. On the insides of some curves, gentle slopes of pebbles look natural.

Rocks jutting from the sides or the bottoms of streams will create interesting eddies. Any

*A stream widens into this placid pond that mirrors the sky and the plantings. Especially fine large stones amid moss and ferns appear to have been placed by nature centuries ago. An Exbury hybrid azalea, a Southern Indica azalea, and Kurume azaleas provide spring color.*

## Pond Construction

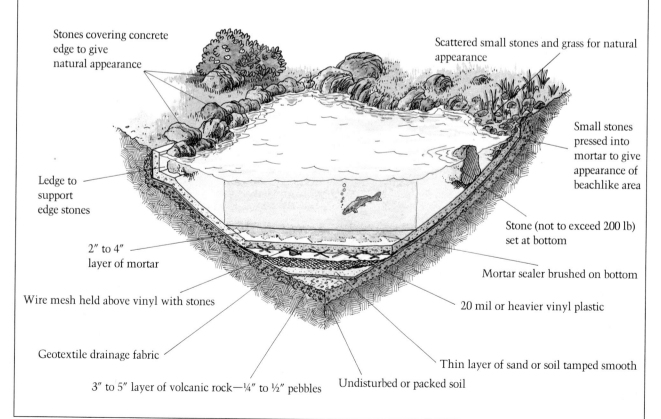

Stones covering concrete edge to give natural appearance

Scattered small stones and grass for natural appearance

Small stones pressed into mortar to give appearance of beachlike area

Ledge to support edge stones

Stone (not to exceed 200 lb) set at bottom

2″ to 4″ layer of mortar

Mortar sealer brushed on bottom

Wire mesh held above vinyl with stones

20 mil or heavier vinyl plastic

Geotextile drainage fabric

Thin layer of sand or soil tamped smooth

3″ to 5″ layer of volcanic rock—¼″ to ½″ pebbles

Undisturbed or packed soil

the sky and refresh visitors. Any garden can have a dry-water feature that suggests a pond as effectively, perhaps, as does water itself.

**Designing a pond**  From the principal viewing point, traditionally the house or the veranda, a pond funnels the eye to the focal point of the garden, usually the waterfall, the mouth of the stream, or the spring that feeds the pond. The funneling function of the pond as it narrows and points toward its apparently remote source is yet another use of the design principle of forced diminishing perspective, discussed in the second chapter (see page 35).

Just as in nature, a pond has a source—a spring or a stream, perhaps with a waterfall— it also has an outlet. In the garden it should emulate its natural counterpart by appearing to have an outlet, even if it is nothing more than a small slope or a flat area with a few rounded stones and marsh grass.

A pond is always asymmetrical, in keeping with the asymmetry of nature. Any asymmetric shape that works is suitable and should include relatively narrow sections where a path can bridge the water.

**Constructing a pond**  In making a pond for your Japanese garden, it isn't enough simply to work out a design, then dig a hole, line it with concrete, surround it with stones and plants, and fill it with water. Without a natural stream flowing through your garden, you will have to provide water. Piped-in water is expensive, and in some areas the supply is low, so it is usually not feasible to allow a continuous stream of water to flow away down the storm drain. Instead, the water must be recirculated.

Without thoughtful, meticulous construction, water will seep through cracks, punctures, or porous concrete and need to be replaced. A perfectly watertight pond loses water through evaporation and must be filled periodically. But a pond or any water feature with even one leak or an unsealed bottom may well empty overnight. The method of construction described below, if followed carefully, should assure a perfect, durable seal.

A number of companies sell heavy vinyl or fiberglass pools or pool kits; some make moderate-sized ponds. You may prefer to build your pond to your own specifications.

For a small pool of no more than about 4 feet in diameter, it is usually sufficient to dig a hole to the desired depth and then sink a container into it. Half of a wine barrel treated to retard rotting, or a galvanized tub painted with very dark gray or black waterproof paint, would be suitable. For a pool no larger than about 6 feet at its widest point, it is sufficient to dig and shape the hole and then line it with 1 inch of mortar sealed with a mortar sealer, obtainable from a masonry supply company. (Choose a sealer that is not toxic to water plants or fish.) Follow the manufacturer's directions carefully, and be sure the sealer covers all the mortar below the water level. You may wish to cover the bottom of the pond with pebbles or gravel.

For a pond, however, a more solid type of construction is desirable. The method explained here has been used with great success by a landscape architect and contractor who specializes in making Japanese gardens. This method of pond construction is appropriate for all ponds in the home garden except those containing stones that weigh more than 200 pounds.

First dig and carefully shape the pond. Its final depth may vary from 8 inches to 24 inches or more. Within the pond, the depth needn't be uniform. Local construction codes often limit the depth of ornamental ponds, so be sure to check the code before starting construction. Most important is a drainage pattern: Be sure that every part of the pond drains and that there is at least a 5-degree slope toward its lowest point, where the pump or drain lies. You may want to build an underwater ledge for supporting edging stones. The ledge may also provide the koi with protection from predators. The bottom should be smooth, with no protruding rocks.

Vinyl sheeting and sealer-coated mortar provide a double seal against leakage. If the soil is sandy or otherwise unstable, line the excavated area with 3 to 5 inches of ¼-inch volcanic rock. Cover the rock with a thin layer of soil or sand. Tamp the soil so that it settles around the rock and makes a 1-inch covering above the surface of the rock. Cover the soil with strips of drainage fabric, a geotextile (one of a class of durable new sheeting products) that provides a soft, virtually puncture-proof buffer for the vinyl liner. It is best to use

**Recirculation System With Submerged Pump**

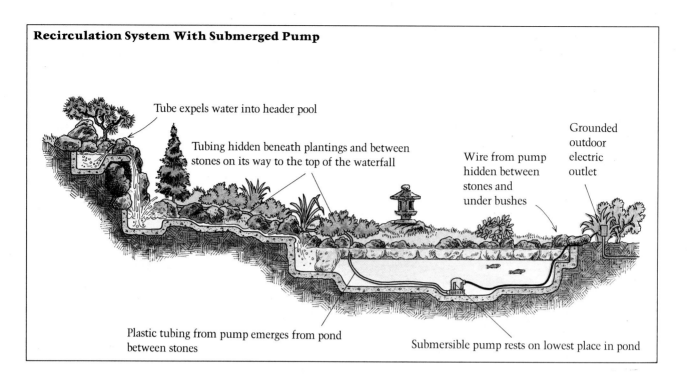

Tube expels water into header pool

Tubing hidden beneath plantings and between stones on its way to the top of the waterfall

Wire from pump hidden between stones and under bushes

Grounded outdoor electric outlet

Plastic tubing from pump emerges from pond between stones

Submersible pump rests on lowest place in pond

at least a 20-mil thick vinyl. Material of this weight is now generally available in 4-foot widths at well-stocked builders' suppliers and from companies that specialize in sheet plastics. Companies that sell the liners can usually make one to your specifications.

Over the liner lay reinforcing wire mesh or steel rebar, the latter if the pond bottom must support heavy stones. Rebar tightly spaced will support more weight than will rebar loosely spaced. Be extremely careful that sharp ends of the mesh or rebar don't puncture the vinyl liner; a single puncture will render the liner useless. Then apply from 2 to 4 inches of mortar which is just wet enough to spread smoothly. You can buy sacks of mortar mix at most builders' supply stores. As a precaution, apply a mortar sealer when the mortar has set. A dark-colored sealer—dark brown or black—will make the pond appear to be deeper, but the natural mortar color is also attractive under water so a clear sealer may be used. The sealer not only reinforces watertightness but prevents toxins from leaching out of the mortar and harming fish or plants. You might also press pebbles or cobbles into the wet mortar, before using the sealer.

**Drains and pumps**   With this method, leaving a hole for a drain or a pump is safe because leakage around its edges is highly unlikely. You have the option of using either a submersible pump and no drain, or of installing a drain useful in draining the pond and in drawing water for the recirculating pump. The drain eliminates the need to camouflage the pipe that leads to the waterfall, as the pipe does not go over the side of the pond but is buried entirely. This method permits the use of a stand pipe, which avoids the possible problem of the lines getting clogged with sediment, dirt, or rocks on the bottom of the pond.

**Filters**   What kind of system is best for collecting and filtering water at the intake end of the pump? For the drainless pond, one of the most efficient is a skeleton of PVC pipe in two diameters, 1 inch or ¾ inch, and ½ inch. A backbone of the large-diameter pipe connects directly to the pump. Secondary ribs of ½-inch pipe reach out into all areas of the pond. Drill the smaller pipes with a standard 3/16-inch bit so that pairs of holes are on either side (rather than on the top and bottom) of the pipes, which lie directly on the pond bottom. Space the pairs of holes closer and closer toward the ends of the ribs. Plug each rib with a regular PVC cap. Glue all joints—at the pump, at each joint where smaller pipes meet the larger pipe, and at each cap. Cover the network of pipes completely with filter cloth, available at building and landscape suppliers. Over the filter cloth spread between 6 and 12 inches of clean gravel. This system, called a

## Recirculation System With Filter Lines

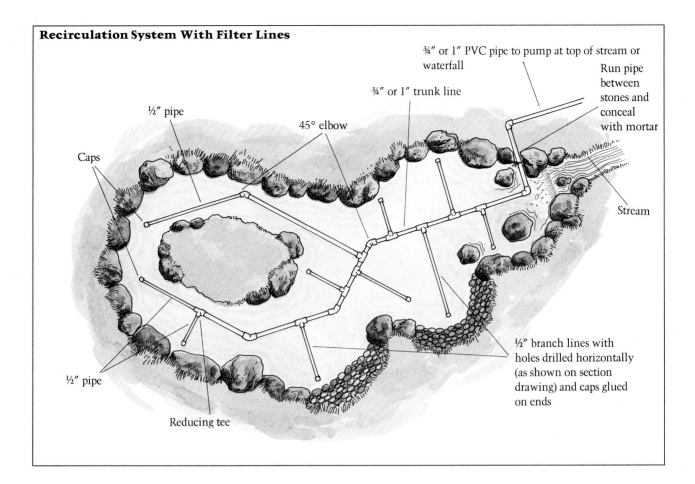

¾″ or 1″ PVC pipe to pump at top of stream or waterfall

Run pipe between stones and conceal with mortar

¾″ or 1″ trunk line

½″ pipe

45° elbow

Caps

Stream

½″ pipe

Reducing tee

½″ branch lines with holes drilled horizontally (as shown on section drawing) and caps glued on ends

## Filter Lines for Recirculation System

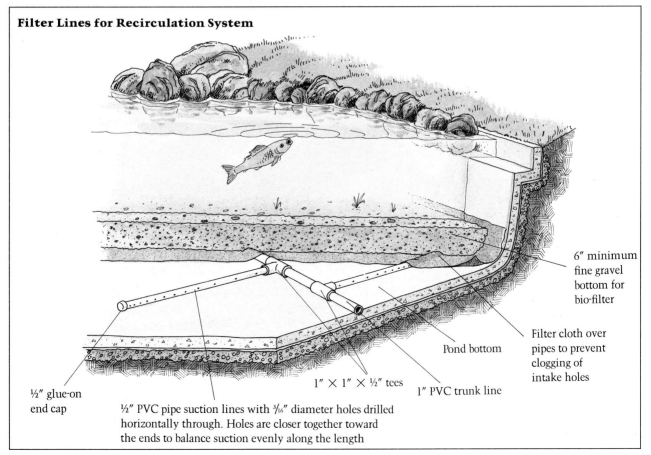

6″ minimum fine gravel bottom for bio-filter

Filter cloth over pipes to prevent clogging of intake holes

1″ PVC trunk line

Pond bottom

1″ × 1″ × ½″ tees

½″ PVC pipe suction lines with ³⁄₁₆″ diameter holes drilled horizontally through. Holes are closer together toward the ends to balance suction evenly along the length

½″ glue-on end cap

*biofilter*, is very effective in drawing water from every part of the pond and thoroughly filtering it. Fill the pond as needed with a garden hose or a line with a conveniently placed valve, from the domestic water supply.

**Pond edges**    Treatments of a pond's edge should harmonize with the garden, suit their particular situations along the edge, and function when necessary as a means of retaining earth. Ornamental edging also serves to camouflage structural edging, the concrete or mortar and plastic of the pond liner. Rarely does a pond have a single, uniform edging. Edgings shift, as in nature, to conform to the configuration of earth and water at any given part of the shore. With whatever edging you choose, care must be taken that drainage from the garden itself doesn't flow into the pond.

Where water is deeper or the bank more precipitous, stones may provide a transition between pond and bank, and if necessary help to retain the bank. Sizes, shapes, and arrangements of stones should be as naturalistically varied and irregular as possible; vegetation may be used to emulate a natural pond edge. The stones look best if most of the tops are low, close to the water, and if the stones aren't piled one on another above water level. Beneath this contrived natural surface, the stones may be attached by mortar to a step or shelf that extends out from the pond lining.

For a shoreline that needs bolstering, you can use wooden pilings—sections of small tree trunks or large limbs, about 3 inches in diameter, preferably weathered rather than raw— driven into the pond's edge. Tops may be of a uniform height or may sit at slightly varying heights. They should make a ragged rather than a smooth line or grouping. This edging has evolved from the old Japanese garden feature of moorings placed near the shore: a few charred, worn, ancient-looking pilings driven into a section of shore, in shallow water.

The pilings must be set in either concrete or mortar, a problem if pond lining is used. Pilings rot, and the alkalinity of mortar or concrete hastens their disintegration. It's virtually impossible to find replacements that will fit perfectly into the vacant holes in the masonry. The old practice of charring pilings has the practical advantage of retarding rot as well as adding patina.

## DRY FEATURES

The design of every water feature described so far in this chapter applies equally well to its dry counterpart that only suggests the presence of water. Dry waterfalls, ponds, and streams, if they are well designed, have much the same aesthetic function and emotional impact as the water features that they resemble.

### Differences Between Wet and Dry Features

Once installed in full-sized gardens, there are, aside from the absence of water, only subtle differences between dry features and the corresponding wet features. There is a significant difference in the construction—for a dry feature, less earth must be moved and nothing needs to be waterproofed—and maintenance, which is easier and far less expensive. An aesthetic difference, perhaps the only one that deserves comment, applies to ponds: A very large dry pond with its lack of movement or reflection and its monotonous expanse can easily seem glaring and unrefreshing; if you plan to make a dry pond, keep its scale modest (but not miniature).

*Above: This dry stream, nestled in the fold of the rolling landscape, aids in channeling runoff during heavy rains. Right: Patterns of precisely raked gravel follow the straight edges of the dry area and the irregular edges of the stone—a stylization of the ripples where water meets stones or shoreline. Below opposite: Stones, a natural-looking deposit of cobbles, and a lush planting of marsh marigold at the edge of the water conceal the lip of the pond. Above opposite: Variously sized stones and a small beach area of cobbles and baby's tears edge the pond.*

*In decomposed granite or very fine, sharp-edged gravel, these handmade Japanese rakes would create sharp-edged patterns. Here, in heavier gravel, they have a softer effect.*

### Raked Sand

The material used most frequently to suggest water is fine raked sand of a special kind. In Japan decomposed granite particles are used. The surfaces of these particles are angular rather than rounded, so they can be shaped into the sharp ridges needed to maintain precisely raked patterns. Earthy, subdued tones make the granite more attractive than white sand as a garden surface. A very fine gravel might be substituted.

**Constructing a raked-sand area** Well-packed earth is the traditional foundation for areas of sand, but mud (which swallows sand) and weeds are potential problems. You can eliminate these problems without creating drainage or anaerobic-bacterial soil conditions—conditions where bacteria which live without oxygen are able to thrive—by laying a porous-fabric weed barrier (one that allows water and air to pass through it) over the ground first and covering it with 2 to 4 or more inches of sand.

Raked patterns are usually stylizations of natural patterns of ripples, eddies, waves, and the smooth flow of water. Whatever their configuration, they suggest movement, from torrential rush to the gentlest purling or subtlest rippling around the edges of banks or stones.

**Maintaining raked areas** Maintenance is minimal where there is little wind and no foot traffic. Evergreen trees and shrubs do not make much litter. Under ideal conditions you will need to rake only every other week. Before you decide on a raked-sand feature, however, be sure of your commitment to regular maintenance: A neglected raked-sand feature is unsightly and out of keeping with the spirit of a Japanese garden. The Japanese use a special wooden rake to maintain the surface, but a steel rake can produce similar results.

## WALLS, FENCES, AND GATES

For privacy, for screening unattractive views, and for creating a sense of intimacy, a Japanese garden is not only enclosed, but also partitioned by walls or fences, or a combination of both. Occasionally earth mounds or trees and shrubs are used for screening or providing a backdrop. Some fences and walls make a solid barrier, others are open and merely suggest divisions or boundaries. Even the most solid enclosures, however, may have dips, gaps, or windows in them for capturing scenery borrowed from surrounding areas. In its appearance and its degree of visual solidity or openness, every successful enclosure or divider perfectly suits the style of the garden and serves its intended purpose.

*This weathered, wooden boundary fence with a stone base is open enough to permit a filtered view beyond and some air circulation, yet it is solid enough to define the boundary strongly and assure privacy.*

Similarly, a gate is stylistically united with its wall or fence as well as with the whole garden. It may offer access to the garden with no sacrifice of privacy or may merely mark a division and provide a transition between parts of a garden, intensifying the intimacy of each part and the sense of mystery that a visitor experiences in looking toward a partly obscured area.

## Boundary Fences

In Japan, boundary fences 7 feet or higher are commonly used to separate a garden from the outside world. They are not only taller but generally more solid, visually and structurally, than dividing fences within a garden. In the United States, local building codes may restrict the height of a fence and require a setback. But even at 5 or 6 feet, a boundary fence usually assures privacy and sets the garden apart. A setback allows room outside the fence for trees or tall shrubs that increase privacy, soften the effect of the fence itself, and from inside create the illusion that the garden extends further outward.

Aside from regulating views from inside and out, a boundary fence makes an acoustical barrier (whose effectiveness can be enhanced by trees or shrubs), blocks wind, and provides some shade.

The styles of boundary fences suitable for residential gardens reflect the simplicity and rusticity of most Japanese gardens and harmonize with the architecture of the house. Natural weathered planks, often charred in places and brushed or sandblasted to accentuate the grain, are frequently used. They are set vertically, alone or in combination with several other materials in any of many patterns, with or without a simple gabled roof. Other materials, used either alone or in combinations, include bamboo (constituting both structural elements and panels fashioned in many different patterns) and plaster covering wood that has been faced with wire mesh, which is sometimes whitewashed but usually earthen. Some fences have stone bases, up to 2 feet high, topped by fencing of other material.

There are many patterns for constructing a boundary fence, from the simplest to those with caps, roofs, or other ornamentation. The appearance of even the simplest fence may be enhanced by a gabled roof. Your fence may be solid or you may have panels to create an open pattern. Horizontal planks or boards will increase the stability of the fence.

## Divider Fences

Within the garden, divider fences, usually smaller and more open than boundary fences,

**Boundary Fence**

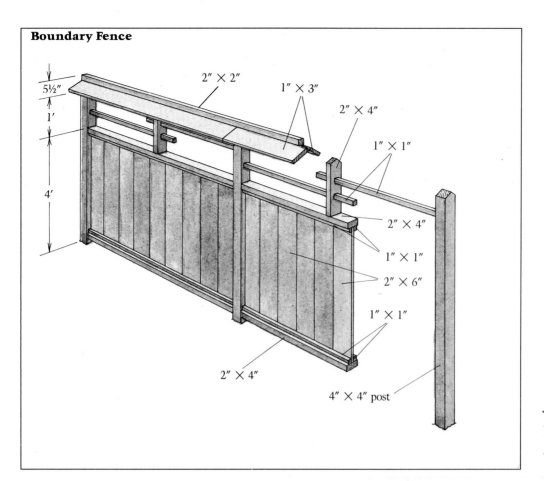

5½"

1'

4'

2" × 2"

1" × 3"

2" × 4"

1" × 1"

2" × 4"

1" × 1"

2" × 6"

1" × 1"

2" × 4"

4" × 4" post

*Weathered wood and bamboo make a semiopen boundary fence that permits glimpses of the wooded area beyond. Asparagus fern softens the base.*

**Divider Fence**

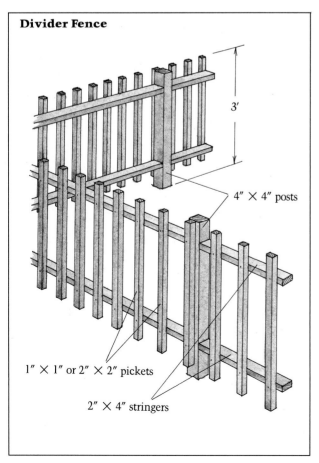

3'

4" × 4" posts

1" × 1" or 2" × 2" pickets

2" × 4" stringers

*Right: This divider fence preserves a sense of intimacy within the garden and defines the entry area. Below left: Skillful placement of this graceful elbow-shaped divider subtly forces the viewer to consider and incorporate the borrowed scenery of the woodland. Flowering dogwood and azalea brighten the scene.*

may serve a number of functions. Principally they set off or define a section of the garden, not by hiding it but by obscuring only part of the area beyond. They are usually low, between 2 and 4 feet in height, and usually between 3 and 6 feet in length. Their open patterns make them gracefully light rather than massive. Solid fences are occasionally used to hide unsightly objects, such as heat pumps, or to make a solid backdrop for a garden accent, setting it off by providing an effective contrast.

Some dividing fences, such as those used as backdrops, may be freestanding. These need vegetation and stones nearby to soften their angularity and help anchor them visually. Others are attached at right angles to the house or another more solid structure. Attached, they are called sleeve fences, are nearly always open in design, made of varying materials (woven bamboo tied to the frame is most common), and have innumerable patterns. A typical sleeve fence is rounded at its outer end. The outer ends of longer ones may taper down to ground level. Sleeve fences create a transition between house and garden.

*This traditional Japanese sleeve fence makes a transition from the angular house to the softer forms of the garden. Set on hinges, the fence doubles as a gate between two sections of the garden.*

*The openness and elegant simplicity of this gate serve to separate sections of this garden. Split bamboo is woven, then tied with natural-fiber cord. The bamboo will weather quickly and appear less conspicuous.*

### Walls

Solid, permanent walls surround many Japanese gardens. Costliest are stone walls, either mortared or dry—that is, carefully crafted of unmortared stones with earth between the stones, so that the walls can be planted with small-scale, perhaps trailing, plants. Mortared stone walls can double as retaining walls for high-mounded earth that slopes down into the garden. Shrubs may be planted on top for added screening, and rocks and even waterfalls may be situated there. Other frequently seen Japanese garden walls are made of plastered clay into which straw has been mixed. Like boundary fences, walls may be capped by gabled roofs.

Many common building materials can be used to make a wall with a pleasing Japanese feeling. Whatever material you decide on, remember that vegetation inside the garden can soften the effect of the wall.

### Gates

Like fences, gates have their uses both at the periphery and inside a garden. Like fences and walls, they can be roofed—even if the fence or wall into which they are built is roofless. Gates range in elaborateness from massive, double-doored outer gates topped with a tile roof, suitable for a large formal garden, to a small, simply roofed, woven-bamboo gate separating sections of a tea garden, to twin upright bark-covered posts with an overhead branch crossing to form a gateway without an actual gate. This gateway will have a particularly Japanese quality if the ends of the crossing branch are allowed to extend beyond the posts, and the tops of the posts allowed to rise above the crossing branch.

Gates should exactly suit the style of the fences within which they stand and should not be embellished with paint and bright or flashy hardware and ornamentation, which are out of keeping with the spirit of Japanese gardens. Outer gates are customarily secured with sliding wooden bolts. Gates intended to remain open should be fitted with discreet latches to prevent them from swinging free.

## STONE GROUPINGS

Stone is so important in every Japanese garden that it has been described as the skeleton, backbone, framework, and foundation of the garden. Garden components which are made from stone, such as stepping stones, bridge anchors, walls, lanterns, and water basins, are discussed later in this chapter. Above all, it is stone used as stone which has the greatest importance in the garden. Placed individually, but far more often in groups, stones are basic to every style of Japanese garden.

Even when used in groups, stones have individual characteristics, and the Japanese will carefully, thoughtfully select every single stone for a garden. Graceful form, attractive color and texture, beauty of vein, and a patina of age are highly valued. Japanese history abounds with accounts of individual garden stones so beautiful that they became fittingly lavish gifts for rulers—or booty for rapacious, powerful men of refined taste.

### Sources of Stones

The choicest stones, to the Japanese, bespeak great age and perfect naturalness. Weathered surfaces, eroded edges, and the organic embellishment of moss and lichen enhance their value. The severe angularity of a fine mountain stone pleases a sophisticated garden maker, especially if the surface has discolored, flaked, acquired some lichen, and lost the stark rawness of a similarly shaped stone

*A single stone and a clump of heartleaf bergenia anchor this stark tree trunk and combine to make a pleasing, balanced composition.*

from a quarry. River rocks whose surfaces have been rounded and smoothed by water have greater beauty than hewn stones. Humble local stones, or stones that resemble local ones so that they harmonize with the natural landscape, are preferable to fine imported ones that bear no natural relation to their new setting. Often, however, suitable local stones are not available, but harmonious imported rocks are. A word of caution: The removal of stones from public or private land without the owner's permission is, in most states, illegal and punishable by fines.

Unless you have easy, legal access to stones from the countryside and the means to transport them, you must go to a commercial supplier. Try to find a company that will allow you to chose each stone, at least each major one, and that will protect the surfaces of stones during delivery, by using nylon webbing or straps (available at drayage or rigging companies) rather than chains, or by putting layers of wood or heavy cardboard between stones and chains or other damaging edges.

## Uses in the Garden

Bear in mind, as you consider stones for your garden, that a stone grouping often serves more than one function. A stone grouping very

seldom stands alone in the garden; to some extent it is usually combined with vegetation. In fact, plants are sometimes shaped to suggest or extend the forms of nearby stones.

Some stone groupings are practical: Stones, together with plants, may conceal a compost pile or a garbage can. Somewhat like sleeve fences, they may suggest divisions of the garden into intimate spaces. And like freestanding dividing fences, they may be combined with greenery to make a backdrop or a composition for a focal feature such as a prized water basin. Often they help to tie down a tall element such as a tree or soften the angularity of and anchor a freestanding fence or a stone bridge. In an open garden area they may help to frame a focal point.

But, most important, groups of stones frequently serve as focal points themselves. They form or help to constitute mountains and real or suggested islands. Or they simply make naturalistic compositions, sometimes with abstract or symbolic overtones.

## Classification by Shape

The Japanese have developed elaborate stone classifications, but five basic shapes suffice to describe stones as they would be used in garden groupings. Smaller stones, of various

**Stone Shapes**

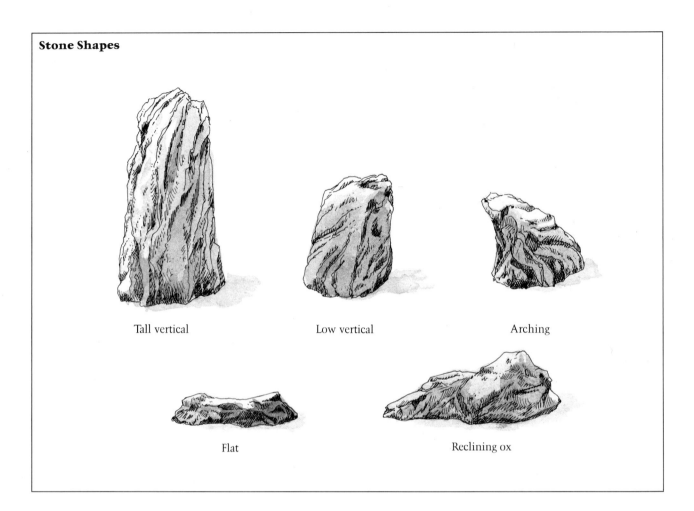

Tall vertical        Low vertical        Arching

Flat        Reclining ox

shapes, called helping stones, fill out and lend naturalistic variety to a grouping.

The three forms of standing, essentially vertical stones are tall vertical, low vertical, and arching.

A tall vertical stone is higher than it is wide and is often the primary stone in a grouping. A low vertical stone may be of any height as long as its width equals or exceeds its height. An arching stone (whose name is also translated "thrusting") may be lower than a low vertical; its top slopes to one side to create a wedge. The slope gives it a strongly directional shape, making it a dynamic component within groupings.

The two essentially spreading forms are flat and reclining (also called reclining ox). A flat stone is just that, flat-topped and low, normally no more than one foot high. Stepping stones are examples of flat stones of small scale. A reclining stone is also essentially horizontal but it is elongated and mounds higher at one end, as the image of a reclining ox suggests.

**Stone Arrangement**

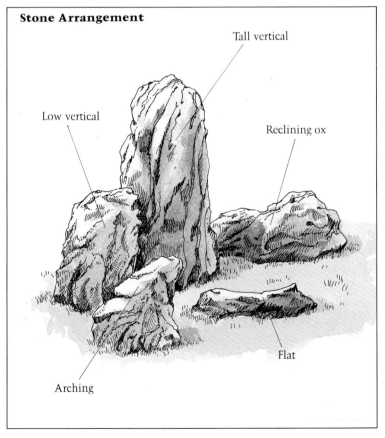

Tall vertical

Low vertical

Reclining ox

Flat

Arching

## Arranging Stones

Over centuries the Japanese have evolved systems of stone placement whose complexity and symbolic significance bewilder Westerners. The basic concepts are, however, straightforward and produce compositions of natural elegance.

Within particular groupings and within particular areas of the garden, use only one type of stone to create the illusion that every stone is native to the garden site. If the stones are layered, arrange them so that their layering is consistent and they are naturalistically tilted, as though they were all projections of the same bedrock. Stones that appear to have been deposited by streams might justifiably look different, but even they should appear to be harmonious with the garden.

Never set stones on the surface of the ground. Bury them as deeply as necessary to make them appear, and to be, strongly anchored. The use of smaller stones and plants around the base of the larger stones can reinforce the appearance of stability. For the same reason, use stones that are larger at the base than at the top.

Use odd numbers of stones. To the three primary stones forming a scalene triangle (see "Using Asymmetric Balance") or other odd numbers of stones, add smaller helping stones. Groupings of five or more major stones begin to take on the proportions of large garden features. Unless that is what you want, limit a grouping to three major stones.

Consider the nature and scale of the garden, and select stones to suit it. The scale of a garden is suggested chiefly by its stones. A fairly large stone or two in a courtyard garden will suggest that the space is larger than it is. The scale of the stones should determine the size of the lanterns, fences, shrubs, and other features close to them.

To create a landscape suggesting a particular landform, use appropriate stones: vertical, angular ones at a mountaintop or the top of a waterfall, for instance, and rounded rocks along a gently inclined lowland stream or a pond. Never lose sight of your overriding purpose: to suggest nature in simplified form.

**Which side is up?**   Before you arrange stones, study each to determine its best side. Determine its natural top, a matter of gravity,

size, and, in some cases, the growth of moss. Usually the heaviest and bulkiest part of the rock is at the bottom. Moss grows on the north side of stone.

**Using asymmetric balance**   The key principle followed in the grouping of stones is that of asymmetric balance, an understanding of which will assure the success of your stone groupings regardless of all the other rules and principles, as long as you are clear on where the lines of view for the arrangement are. As a general rule, arrange major stones in threes, in a scalene triangle or an interlocking system of scalene triangles. Unless there is only one viewing point, think three-dimensionally, considering the depth of the grouping and its appearance from each viewing point, as well as its face-on appearance from the main viewing point.

Study your site, your stones, and your viewing points. Then sketch the possibilities that occur to you. Before you dig away earth to place the first stone, have a diagram—even if your plan changes while you are working.

**Moving and setting stones**   Where do you start? Which stone or unit of stones do you place first, to be followed by which one, and so on, not just in one group but in a garden area or an entire garden?

One method is to move from most to least important, an especially sensible sequence

*A tall vertical, a low vertical, and a reclining-ox stone combine to create a composition that is pleasingly balanced from any angle. Surrounding touches of vegetation soften the effect. The arrangement echoes other garden features—particularly the decaying tree trunks that were intentionally left in order to lend a sense of time and of the cycles of nature.*

when large stones are limited in number and therefore should be used only in important focal positions. Another sequence concerns only groupings that are to include large stones to be placed by truck and derrick: Move from the stone or grouping most distant from the place where a truck with a derrick would enter the site to the closest, so the placed stones won't get in the way as the rest are being positioned.

Any damage to natural surface diminishes or destroys a stone's usefulness in the garden. To insure that stones weighing several hundred pounds or more reach their final positions in your garden undamaged and in proper alignment, make some preparations. Unless you're adept at heavy construction, hire a fully qualified contractor, for your sake and that of the stones.

If you do the work yourself, use a wooden lever rather than a crowbar on any surface that won't be buried or otherwise hidden, to avoid scarring. Protect surfaces by using as much padding as needed. If necessary, use a block or a winch, or a derrick mounted on the rear of a truck.

Except in a dry-stream garden, where an unburied stone might suggest the continual shifting of stones by the force of the stream, bury each stone deep enough that it seems to be growing out of the earth. After careful measurement, dig a hole for each stone, and compact the earth inside the hole until it is firm and the bottom is at the intended depth. If the stone will be rolled by lever rather than lowered into place, dig away the wall on the side of the hole where the stone will enter, and replace earth as needed afterward.

## PATHS, STEPS, AND BRIDGES

With the exception of courtyard gardens, Japanese gardens invite viewers to walk through them. Stepping stones in the outer tea garden lead visitors away from everyday concerns into a realm of quietude; the stroll-garden path invites visitors to set out on foot to savor the garden's subtleties and explore its mysteries. In any walked-in garden, a side path may reveal to the curious visitor a choice feature.

The path, or a system of paths, provides firm, dry, safe footing; directs and paces the visitor; and protects planted, raked, or other prepared or detailed surfaces. If sensitively designed and carefully constructed, paths become not just the route through, but a part of, the garden's beauty and spirit.

Paths range in elaborateness and formality from wide, elegantly paved stone walkways, to stepping-stone pathways, to the simplest of packed-earth trails. One garden may contain forms of all three. Changes of level call for steps, and wet or dry streams too wide for stepping stones call for bridges.

### Trails

The most rudimentary form of paths, trails require little effort or material to make. Their simplicity complements the naturalism of the Japanese garden. Trails that are both dressed and contained are far stronger architecturally and are thus less naturalistic.

**Basic trails** Paths at their most basic look as though the constant passage of feet (or hoofs, or paws) has worn them into the earth. They seem nature's own creation—this is their chief asset in a style of garden whose purpose is to suggest nature and summon its spirit. In even a highly crafted, formal garden, trails can lend intimacy to the quietest, most secluded areas.

Trails do have their drawbacks. In wet weather they become muddy; in dry weather they are dusty. Inevitably trails encourage the growth of weeds.

To make a trail, wet the soil to a depth of several inches, allow it to drain, then with a shovel or hoe remove 2 or 3 inches of soil along with any rocks and weeds. A comfortable trail width is about 3 feet wide, but a variable width can regulate pace (walkers tend to slow down in the wide spots) and enhance the naturalistic feeling. Contour the trail so that water drains to the sides and away, and be sure to pack the soil firmly.

**Dressed trails** By dressing trails with bark, pine needles, composted sawdust, gravel, or crushed rock, mud is eliminated, dust minimized, and weeds reduced, although it is difficult to keep all dressings entirely free of weeds and fallen leaves. Where soil freezes, buckles, and then thaws into mud, a covering is even more useful. All dressings need to be replenished periodically. Bark, sawdust, and

**Nobedan Path**

**Path on Slope**

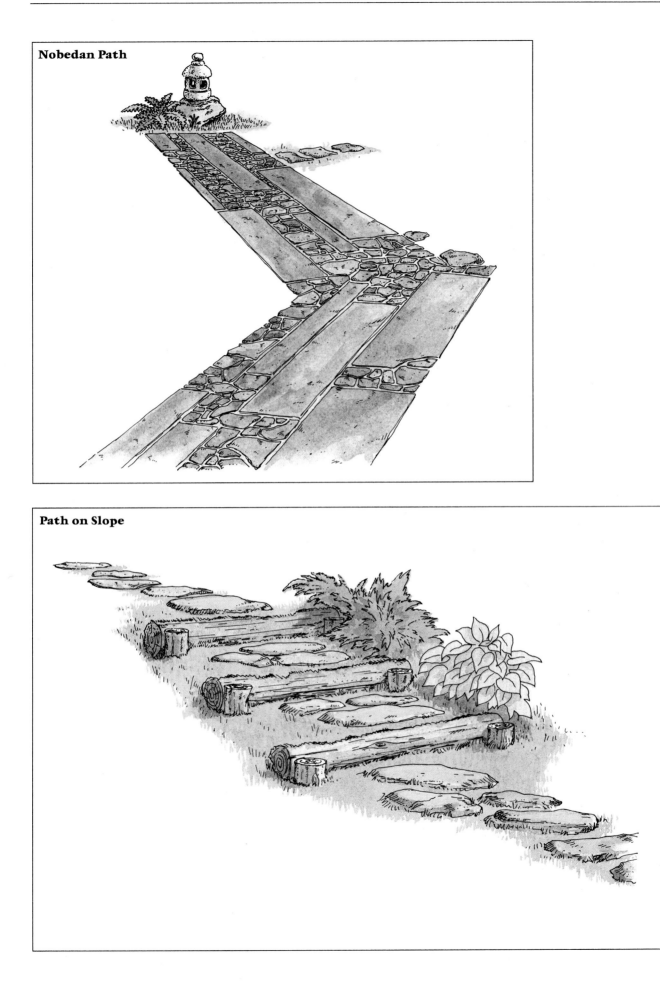

pine needles decay; dry sawdust blows away; gravel and bark get kicked off the path.

Gravel, with its rounded surfaces, provides an unstable footing if it is much more than one inch deep. Eventually gravel and even crushed rock will pack down into the earth, although a fabric weed barrier can retard or eliminate this problem as will a generous layer of decomposed granite. Crushed rock (the ½-inch size) offers a firm footing. As it settles, pieces lock into place. In Japan the slushy sound of gravel and the muted crunching of crushed rock underfoot are considered delightful sensory additions to a garden.

**Contained trails** You can install header boards and make a more durable, less troublesome dressed pathway, if you aren't set on a trail that looks natural. A contained trail allows you to use a weed barrier or decomposed granite more neatly and easily, and it keeps most loose particles of dressing within bounds. You can minimize the formality of such a path by encouraging ground cover to hide the header board and to make the path's width appear random. Or you can make a broad, formal gravel path (use ¼-inch gravel) contained

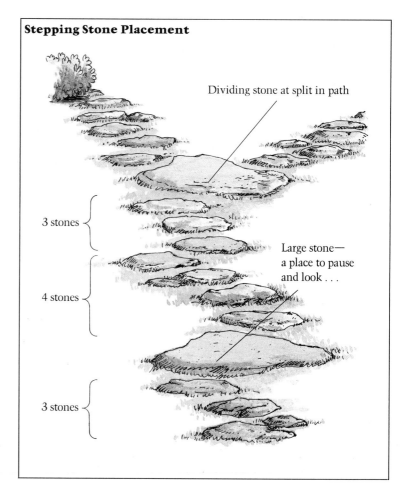

**Stepping Stone Placement**

Dividing stone at split in path

3 stones

4 stones

Large stone— a place to pause and look . . .

3 stones

*An informal, inconspicuously bordered gravel trail changes level through the use of logs and stakes, which hold the gravel in place. Notice how the header board is sometimes obscured by low vegetation, so that the path seems random in width and blends with its surroundings. New foliage of pieris 'Flame of the Forest' makes a brilliant accent.*

by visible header boards, or by concrete or stone strips as is done in many of the large gardens of Japan. When you lay out a trail, pay attention to contouring and topography to assure that no puddles will form.

### Stepping Stones

Most popular in Japanese residential gardens and in Japanese-style American ones are paths of *tobi-ishi*, or stepping stones. Since the development of the tea garden, stepping-stone paths have been considered practical and pleasing. Most stepping stones are used on dry land, but they can cross streams and ponds. Some blend so well with their surroundings that they are unobtrusive; others are intentionally fashioned and arranged to create formal effects. Sizes vary but generally stepping stones are between 15 and 20 inches across, requiring strollers to walk alone or in single file. Stone surfaces (smooth to slightly uneven) and, more commonly, the size, spacing, and pattern of arrangement permit the skilled garden maker to guide visitors toward a greater appreciation of the garden by

directing their route and their pace as they walk through it. The design principle of hide-and-reveal may be achieved by this controlled pacing of the stroller.

**Patterns**  Occasionally stepping stones are laid out formally; more often their configurations are natural in appearance. Close to the house, symmetrical stones are sometimes formed into straight or angled lines, but asymmetrical arrangements are far more usual as they echo the apparent randomness of other garden components. Instead of spanning the shortest distance between two points, stones usually meander. Their Japanese name, *tobi-ishi*, which means flying stones, refers to traditional patterns of arrangement that emulate the flight patterns of various wild birds. Other, nonrepresentational patterns are simple, approximating S curves and gracefully distorted V shapes. The possibilities are many and varied.

**Positioning**  The traditional rules for setting stones in place, in any pattern, take into

*Above left: Large, smooth, evenly spaced stepping stones provide sure footing and permit rapid movement through this garden area. Above right: Stones are placed close together in the manner of nobedan, but the walkway varies in width. The jigsaw puzzle of carefully chosen and placed stepping stones creates a nearly continuous smooth surface, although the stones are just uneven enough to prevent the stroller from hurrying. Vegetation of this young garden will eventually fill the open areas adjacent to the walkway and soften its effect.*

account the considerations of beauty, safety, and the comfort of the stroller.

Space stones about 4 inches apart. Stones crossing water need to be placed closer. Where you want to hurry the strollers along, space stones further apart but not so far that footing is unstable when stones are wet. Where you want the strollers to slow down, space stones more tightly. Similarly, uneven spacing slows the gait; even spacing usually accelerates it. Stones placed with insufficient regard for spacing and ease of walking will distract the strollers, making them feel as if they were playing hopscotch rather than viewing a garden. Determine the positioning of your stones before beginning to construct the path by laying out and walking over newspapers folded to the size of the stepping stones.

Bury each stone so that it stands at the same height above ground level as every other stone in the path, somewhere between 1½ and 3 inches high. The top surface of each should be perfectly level.

Lay the largest stones first. As a general rule, let the largest stones span the axis of the path and the smallest lie away from the axis. Where one stepping-stone path forks or intersects another, place a large dividing stone to give visual and practical stability to the intersection. At sharp turns in the path, use large stones for sound, comfortable footing. Wherever you want the stroller to pause and look around, place a large stone.

Position every stone so that its length is perpendicular to the axis of that segment of the path. Not only will the stone look more stable, but it will be easier to step on than if it were parallel to the axis.

In working out a sequence for stones, place together stones whose edges are almost but not quite parallel over the greatest length possible: a flat (or nearly flat) side next to a flat side, a convexity matching a concavity, a protruding angle matched to a recessed one. Of course, all such shapes relate approximately, not exactly. Wherever two stones cannot be placed together to match, add one or more small secondary stones, whose function is not necessarily to be stepped on but to complete the design.

**Stability** Stones that move when stepped on are unsafe. Stepping on an unstable stone, even without accident, will interrupt the contemplation of the stroller. If a stepping-stone path must bear much weight (a wheelbarrow, for example) make it especially stable. And, to avoid discomfort and danger, be sure that each stone is set at exactly the same height above ground, as detailed earlier, or at gradually increasing or decreasing heights when on slopes.

Bulky stones set deep and solidly into the ground will create stability. Beneath the three inches or less of exposed stone may lie 1 foot or more of buried stone. Stepping stones sold in this country are usually shallow. If you can't obtain deep stones, anchor every shallow, potentially unstable stone in a buried pocket of concrete: For each stone, dig a hole several inches deep and fill it with concrete. When the concrete has set, attach the stepping stone with mortar, making sure that the surface along the path is level. A far simpler and equally stable method is to put 2 inches of sand in the hole and tamp the stone firmly into the sand.

**Stepping-stone substitutes** In the United States, where stepping stones are in short supply and nearly always expensive, some widely available substitutes are both serviceable and attractive.

Wooden rounds—cross sections of redwood, cypress, or cedar trunks—cost relatively little. Proper treatment with copper naphthenate or other preservatives extends their life. Once they have weathered, their appearance harmonizes with the rest of a Japanese garden. Drawbacks of wooden rounds are their limited lifespan (no more than a decade and usually far shorter), their tendency to split, and their light weight, which makes them less stable than stone. Using the largest rounds for maximum stability, set them into a bed of sand, gravel, or earth so that their tops are just slightly above the surface.

Geometric precast exposed aggregate stepping stones, sold at nurseries and garden supply stores, are heavier and more stable but less natural looking. They sit in the ground like true stepping stones, but their uniform appearance limits their use in a Japanese garden. You may also want to consider the limited use of sunken adobe or concrete blocks.

You can make a satisfactory substitute for true stepping stones with mortar or concrete. Poured in place, mortar stepping stones are as permanent as stone and, if properly finished, they resemble stone. You can vary the shapes endlessly for a very naturalistic walkway. Dig and shape a hole at least 3 inches deep for each stepping stone, tamp the earth, and press a 4- or 5-inch-wide strip of metal flashing around the edges of the hole to create a form. Rub the inside surface of the flashing with mineral oil. Pour enough concrete to cover the bottom of the hole. On top of the concrete lay a cut-to-order piece of wire mesh (stucco wire is suitable) for reinforcement, then pour more mortar into the form. Be sure the mortar mix is thick enough to hold its shape when the form is removed. Remove the form. Use a trowel to round the edges and contour the stone. After five or six hours, depending on climatic conditions, use a paint brush and water to whisk away the surface "cream," exposing the gritty surface for better traction and a more natural appearance. Timing is important: If you wait too long, the cream will have hardened, and if you whisk too soon, you will mar the mortar. So experiment before you attempt pouring a whole path of stones.

### Paved Walkways

Among the most elegant features of many traditional Japanese gardens are *nobedan.* Contrasting with the predominant naturalism of a garden, these paved stone walkways of a uniform, generous width add a formal, architectural note. A paved walkway may lie close to the house, at an entrance or parallel to a veranda, or constitute a major thoroughfare across broad, open areas of the garden. Stepping stones and trails dictate that strollers walk alone or in single file, while paved walkways are often wide enough so that people are able to stroll together. A uniform or nearly uniform surface allows strollers to pay less attention to their footing and more attention to the scenery around them. Variations on traditional forms provide endless possibilities for gardens in the United States.

**Materials and patterns** Whether laid out with parallel borders of granite curbing stone or unbordered, a nobedan-style path has straight, parallel sides. Angles rather than curves mark changes in direction. Many possibilities for paving materials fall within these formal guidelines. Patterns and textures may reinforce the symmetry or create random, natural effects that link the path with the predominant naturalism of the garden.

Most paved walkways combine stones of symmetrical and natural shapes. For example, large rectangular granite slabs may be combined with flat-surfaced river stones of random (or of more or less uniform) size.

A variation on the nobedan effect is the walkway, or segment of walkway, consisting of two long rectangular strips of granite called label stones because of their resemblance in shape to the Japanese cards, known as labels, on which poems are written. Laid parallel and nearly touching, the strips overlap for approximately two fifths their length.

*This classic nobedan-style path carries the formality of the house into the garden. The walkway changes direction with angles rather than with curves. Unlike many nobedan, this one is made entirely, rather than partly, of geometric stones.*

enough to call for two slabs, rarely three or more. Supporting rocks or rock piers hold the slabs securely where they join. Double- or single-span bridges that are made up of one or more pairs of cut, parallel slabs placed close together tend to look more secure.

If you can't find stone slabs or want to avoid their considerable cost, substitute precast concrete slabs whose color and texture are subdued and stonelike. Because precast concrete slabs are heavy and unwieldy, you may want to call in a professional to deliver and set them into place.

**Plank bridges**  Heavy plank bridges are as simple and natural looking as stone slabs. They may be used as slabs are used. Unlike stone-slab bridges, plank bridges need no anchor stones.

A popular style of plank bridge is the low, zigzagging *yatsuhashi* bridge. Rather than taking them directly across the water, the yatsuhashi bridge causes strollers to move slowly and indirectly, and leads them to contemplate the views to be seen as they cross.

Many patterns may be created with planks, laid singly or parallel. One example is a bridge of two parallel timbers, 4 inches by 4 inches, or larger, supporting closely spaced rails or boards laid across the timbers and nailed down securely. Use pressure- or preservative-treated wood throughout and, where they will come in contact with water or soil, cover the supporting rails with vinyl or some other form of plastic sheeting.

**Earth bridges**  Bridges of wood and earth, called *dobashi*, are either flat or arched. Structurally they are similar to a rail bridge. For supporting timbers, use straight logs or curving ones to give the bridge a gentle arch. Cover them with rails—that is, smaller logs, 3 to 4 inches in diameter—placed as close together as possible and nailed down securely. For durability, lay 1 to 2 inches of clay over the rails and pack it down. Make parallel 4-inch mounds of soil mixed with sand, spanning the bridge at its outer edges. Between the mounds spread an even layer of sand and soil, about 3 inches deep, and pack it firmly. Plant the mounds with a dense, low, perennial grass. Or instead of grassy mounds, use tightly tied bundles of reeds to edge the bridge. Another

form of earth bridge can also be grassed over: rolls of living turf are laid over the layers of clay and earth. Some earth bridges may be heavy enough to require trestles in the middle for support. Again, use treated wood wrapped in vinyl to insure durability for the supporting portions of the bridge.

## GARDEN ACCENTS
Many traditional Japanese garden artifacts and embellishments are more than merely ornamental. Actually or symbolically, they may provide comfort or convenience. Especially in an American garden in the Japanese style, however, their presence is justified if they merely enhance the garden's serenity. They look best when only a few are used.

### Lanterns
Zen priests and tea masters popularized stone-garden lanterns (*ishi-doro*) by incorporating them into tea gardens. Lanterns of stone (but occasionally of wood, bamboo, or bronze) are now the single most common artifact to be found in the gardens of Japan and are used, not to light the garden at night, but to contrast pleasingly and subtly with natural features.

*Above: A layer of lengthwise planks atop a base of crosswise logs makes a simple, solid bridge. The logs add to the rustic appearance. A Japanese crabapple is flowering. Opposite above left: The rusticity of this stone lantern with an informal, almost primitive design is enhanced by a covering of moss. Opposite above right: The lines of this formal lantern— placed to light a pathway—are temporarily softened by a covering of snow. Opposite below: Nestled among the rocks and low water plants at the edge of a pond, this rough-hewn lantern seems to be made from the native stone.*

Although many lanterns are never actually lit, they are properly placed in the garden wherever light would be useful: for example, along walkways, especially where turns or shifts in level occur, near boat docks (real or suggested), at gateways, near bridges or water-spanning stepping stones, or near a water basin. They are also used to complete compositions of stones, or of stones and plants, to mark the edge of a pond, or to create reflections from an island in the pond.

The Japanese value highly the appearance of great age in a lantern and have developed methods of giving a patina of age to new lanterns: smearing them with snail secretions or bird droppings and keeping them in shade and frequently moistened, until moss or lichen takes ahold. Occasional rubbing with dirt or humus may produce the same result.

Lanterns imported from Japan are sold in the United States, some for several hundreds or thousands of dollars. A graceful stone lantern nearly always justifies its expense, but a good concrete one of a rustic design makes a pleasing addition to most garden spots.

If you want to light your lantern, insert a firebox of paraffin and a wick, or use a candle.

*This unusually refined, large chozubachi rests on a bed of gravel to keep the surrounding ground from becoming muddy. Over time, exposure to the elements will weather the chozubachi, blending it with its surroundings.*

*This refined tsukubai is surrounded by all of the accessories typically found in a tea garden. This tsukubai is most unusual, however, because it is combined with a deer scare. Water from the slender bamboo pipe on the left fills the receptacle of the larger bamboo pipe, causing it to tip and strike the edge of the basin with a sharp crack as it empties.*

*A fascinating assortment of koi swim in the carefully filtered, clean water at a narrow end of a large pond.*

Or, if you use a low-wattage bulb, you can wire your lantern. Cover the windows with rice paper or another, similar translucent material.

## Water Basins

Like lanterns, water basins are nearly always of stone, and most highly prized are ancient ones of simple, rustic design. The water basin, or *tsukubai*, appeared in Japanese gardens as an adjunct to the tea ceremony, to be used by guests for washing their hands and mouths in a ritual of purification before they entered the tea house.

A typical tsukubai is low, requiring that the user stoop. A bamboo ladle often sits on the stone, and the reservoir in the top of the basin may either be filled by hand or fed by a bamboo pipe that drips water into it. Even if the basin never fulfills its original function in a garden, its appearance, enhanced by the sound of dripping water and the rippling, reflective surface of the water, makes it a splendid accent.

Most styles are extremely naturalistic—a scooped-out stone is the most common—but some are more architectural. The more refined styles have names such as square star, oven-shaped, priest's scarf, and Chinese junk.

Surrounding the tsukubai are auxiliary stones that make a functional arrangement. In front of the basin is a stone to stand or kneel on. To its right is a stone on which a pitcher or kettle might be set. To the left of the water basin, a protection stone, nearly as large as the basin stone, shields the area to its left from splashing water and may also accommodate a portable lamp. An underlying bed of gravel prevents muddiness.

In a tea garden, the water basin is placed close to the tea house. When placed outside the tea garden, it may lie near the house, probably next to the veranda, where it would be taller. This type of water basin is called a *chozubachi*. In a Japanese-style American garden, a water basin may be placed wherever it is in keeping with its surroundings.

Like stone lanterns, authentic Japanese water basins are expensive. A well-designed concrete basin will cost far less. A bamboo *kakeki*, or flume, is simple to make and may be attached to plumbing or connected to a concealed garden hose. A small recirculating pump can also keep water flowing.

## Deer Scare

The deer scare, or *shishi odoshi*, has agricultural origins: Farmers used it to frighten away deer or other animals that threatened their crops. Water flows out of a bamboo pipe and down into a lip reservoir that is a length of bamboo set on a pivot. When the reservoir is full, the weight of the water tips the length of bamboo abruptly downward. With a loud *clack* it strikes a rock, the water tips out and the reservoir swings back up. The rhythm is as regular as the flow of water and it introduces pleasing sounds to the garden.

In your garden you may decide to use a shishi odoshi (also called a *sozu*) near the edge of a pond, where the runoff can be channeled or will furnish the water for a tiny, intermittent cataract that would run down a rock face. A small recirculating pump might be used to provide the water.

## Koi

One of the most refreshing experiences that a Japanese garden can offer is the chance to feed the koi. These brilliant relatives of the common goldfish, prized for their colorful patterns, are a kind of carp. Like a special garden stone, a magnificently patterned koi is considered a treasure and such a specimen may cost thousands of dollars. The choicest forms of *nisiki koi* (brocaded koi) are too costly for most home gardens, but less costly forms are available. Given time and the right conditions, koi can grow to two or three feet in length and may live for decades.

If you want koi in your garden, you must provide them with proper pond conditions. Water must be effectively filtered and well aerated. Some fresh water must be added every few days, or continuously. If predators such as raccoons come into your garden, part of your pond must be deep enough, or protected by an overhang, so that the koi are safe. Partial shade is necessary, and there should be enough volume of water, along with ample depth, to prevent abrupt temperature changes and to keep temperatures low enough to prevent too rapid a growth of algae. If your pond does not have a biofilter (see page 48), some other type of filtration system is necessary. Determine exactly what special requirements your local climate imposes on the maintenance of koi in a garden pond.

# Plants

*Plants are nearly always included in Japanese gardens, but their functions often differ dramatically from those of plants in occidental gardens. So, in several respects, do their placement, training, and maintenance.*

This chapter offers some basic principles of plant selection and use and instructions for giving certain plants the care they require in Japanese gardens. The plant charts list a broad sampling of appropriate plants, including traditional Japanese favorites and suitable alternatives. Although bonsai plants are not a feature of traditional Japanese garden styles, a discussion of their adaptation, use and maintenance in Japanese-inspired gardens is included.

An understanding of which plants are horticulturally and aesthetically compatible provides you with a basis for selection and planting. Practically and aesthetically, appropriateness is the key to sound plant selection and use. Reliable regionalized books and knowledgeable local nursery staff or landscape consultants can help you choose plants.

Besides the basic, practical considerations of size, scale, and general appropriateness, there are aesthetic considerations. The shape and size of plants may, to some extent, be controlled; their color cannot. You will need to know the colors of plants (including shades of green) and their textures in order to choose knowledgeably. You will also need to know what plants and combinations of plants would contribute to the Japanese spirit of restraint and subtlety.

The primary purpose of a Japanese garden is to suggest, through creating repose, universal harmony. Appropriately chosen and placed plants will support this purpose.

*This dramatic sheet of cherry plum (*Prunus cerasifera 'Hollywood'*) blossoms provides a glowing backdrop for the composition of stones, evergreen shrub, and small gnarled tree. Note how the* Pittosporum tobira *has been shaped to echo the form and slope of the stones.*

## APPROPRIATE PLANT SELECTION AND USE

Appropriate plant selection—both species and size of specimens—is essential to creating and maintaining your intended garden effect. Consider how easy or difficult a particular species is to keep at the desired size and shape. Planting design for Japanese gardens depends upon complete control over the size and shape of each plant. The quality of a garden depends on the plantings' being maintained at a certain scale. The smaller the garden, the more stringent the control will need to be.

In choosing, you must decide whether to plant a young tree or shrub and wait for it to reach optimal size before your garden reaches the form you want and whether you will be able to keep the plant at the size you want.

The overall Japanese garden plant selection is unified, and plants are used singly and in combinations to give the impression of the natural world. This means they suit the garden and the places where they are planted within it, and groupings of plants are aesthetically compatible.

Appropriate in a Japanese garden is a gracefully naturalistic placement of plants, which are arranged as stones are arranged. Their apparent randomness looks natural and therefore appropriate. Three plants used in a grouping are likely to look more natural than would two or four; a scalene triangle looks far less studied than an equilateral one, and certainly less than a row, a circle, or a rectangle. Observe the random patterns of plant distribution in nature before you arrange plants in your Japanese garden.

## USE OF PLANTS TO CREATE ILLUSION

In the light of the design principles discussed in the second chapter, you will appreciate that the selection and placement of plants have everything to do with how the eye of the beholder can be directed to focus on some garden areas or details and to gloss over others. Japanese garden design relies heavily on optical illusion and plant use is instrumental in creating or reinforcing such effects.

### Background

Begin with an evaluation of the background greenery in your garden. In any garden the

background screens out unsightliness. In Japanese gardens, in which a sense of apartness from the world beyond is usually a basic objective, not only is the world beyond usually hidden (with the exception of borrowed scenery, discussed earlier) but the background of the visible scene encourages the eye to move to focal points within it.

Because the eye gravitates naturally to dark spots in the landscape, evergreen shrubs or plants that create deep shadows will emphasize a focal point situated in front of them. The eye moves to the focal point and is held there by the contrast with the background darkness.

In a typical courtyard garden, and in some gardens of other Japanese styles, background greenery can delude the eye in a different way. Its primary function is to suggest that the garden extends beyond the confines of what is seen, that there is more around the corner. A dense planting of tall bamboo

*The scene is a study in the subtleties of a green color scheme. The native vine maple (Acer circinatum) planted behind the lantern complements the larger Japanese maple above.*

*Apparent randomness characterizes this entryway planting. Even the three carefully shaped pyracanthas look natural. Japanese aucuba provides contrasts. The evergreen Belgian Indica azaleas and Kurume azalea provide color.*

*The background of deep and medium greens draws the eye to the relatively bright vertical stone.*

toward one side of the far wall of a garden, for example, hides the actual corner, and the feathery foliage and willowy habit of the bamboo seem open rather than wall-like and final.

### Depth

By manipulating the fore-, middle, and background of a scene, Japanese garden makers use plants to deepen a cramped or shallow garden or make an already sizeable garden seem even deeper. Large plants placed in the foreground with smaller ones in the background can create a forced diminishing perspective that makes the space seem deeper than it actually is.

This effect can be greatly enhanced by obscuring the middle ground. For instance, if you position a large Japanese umbrella pine in the foreground, near the viewing point, and a planting of nandina shrubs and Japanese boxwood (comparatively small shrubs) in the background, you have set up a forced dimin-

ishing perspective which causes the area to appear deeper than it is. But that forced perspective may not be very convincing unless you somehow break the smooth connection between the foreground and the background. The middle ground, perhaps a flat area of moss or ground cover, should include something that would catch the eye and further distance the background without in any way blocking it. Low, rounded stones interplanted with compact shrubs—for example, Kurume azaleas, whose shape reinforces the shape of the stones—would interrupt the smooth, low middle ground and break the connection.

Texture and tone can also create or enhance the illusion of distance. Bold texture in the foreground and fine texture in the background stretch space; dark green in the foreground and lighter or softer tones of green in the background create the same effect by making the background seem part of a hazy, distant place.

## A SAMPLING OF PLANTS

The charts that follow include, in several categories, plants suitable for Japanese gardens. No attempt has been made to present an exhaustive list of every popular and appropriate plant; such a list would be the material for an entire book. The charts are meant to suggest, wherever possible, at least one plant in each category suitable to each climate area of the United States and to give a sense of the range of possibilities in texture, color, seasonal variety, size, and distinguishing characteristics. The charts, weighted toward species adaptable in broad climate ranges, include many traditional Japanese favorites and a number of suitable North American and other non-Japanese species whose visual and horticultural qualities suit them to various uses in Japanese-style gardens.

### Names

Plants within each category are alphabetized by their universally accepted Latin names. The most widely used common name of each is included parenthetically. A few plants here have no common names.

### Hardiness Zones

Every plant listed is keyed to a map of climate zones published by the U.S. Department of Agriculture (see page 107). Zones are determined by their average minimum temperatures, so the map is a key to cold hardiness. Some areas in a given zone are warmer or colder than the overall zone.

### Deciduous or Evergreen

In Japanese gardens, as in all gardens, which plants are used and how is determined partly by whether they shed their leaves (or die back, if they are deciduous perennials) or remain evergreen. This information is included for each entry. Because evergreens are essential to the restrained color schemes and are the backbone of year-round greenery essential to Japanese garden design, many of the plants listed are evergreen.

### Height

The height of a plant is important in planning any garden. Because Japanese gardens rely heavily on maintaining plant scale to attain particular and overall effects, garden heights (as opposed to heights in the wild, under ideal conditions, or perhaps after decades or centuries) are listed. Garden heights are heights that can be maintained by pinching or pruning. Listings of species with recommended cultivars differing in height include the word *variable*. To indicate an unusual range of heights possible with and without pruning, as with *Pinus thunbergiana*, upper and lower figures are given.

### Special Ornamental Value

To assist you in determining what ornamental purposes a species can (or cannot) serve in your garden, the chart lists whether the plant has showy flowers, ornamental fruit or seeds, attractive green foliage, autumn color, or an especially appealing habit or branch pattern.

### Comments

Further information about particular assets (and, occasionally, drawbacks) of a species, notable cultivars or close relatives, special needs, and unusual uses, is given here.

## LARGE TREES AND SHRUBS

This large and diverse category is especially important because of the prominence of these plants when used as specimens. A few plants listed here may be used to form screens or high, sheared hedges, to provide a background for focal features—for example, Japanese cedar, holly, sweet olive, pittosporum, and Canadian hemlock. For pointers on training and pruning, see page 91.

Many trees and shrubs may be used effectively in the foreground or the background, depending upon the effect you would like. Traditionally, brightly flowering, large deciduous plants are placed away from viewing points. The seasonally dramatic flowering cherry tree is a notable exception (because of its special emotional connotations to the Japanese) and may be used wherever its form and mass fit into a garden design. Dense evergreens or deciduous trees reinforced by evergreens are used most often as background. If a species can be seen beyond the confines of the garden, it is customarily included within the plan of the garden itself as well, for continuity.

*Opposite left: star magnolia makes a brilliant early-spring garden accent. Because it grows slowly, it is a sensible choice if you want a tree that will stay within the bounds of desired size without requiring much pruning.*
*Opposite above right: flowering dogwood 'Rubra' brings soft spring color to the understory of this woodland garden. Later in the season it will shade and lend intimacy to this composition of stones and gravel. In fall it will make a brief show of red foliage.*
*Opposite below right: This Japanese maple has been carefully pruned to control its size and to shape its boughs into parallel planes.*

| | Hardy to U.S.D.A. Zone | Deciduous/Evergreen | Height | Special Ornamental Value | Flowers | Fruit or Seed | Green Foliage | Fall Foliage | Habit/Branching Pattern |
|---|---|---|---|---|---|---|---|---|---|
| **LARGE TREES AND SHRUBS (12 feet or more)** | | | | | | | | | |
| *Acer ginnala* (Amur maple) | 3 | D | 20′ | • | • | • | • | | Multitrunked unless pruned to single trunk. Red-winged seed contrast with green foliage in late summer. |
| *Acer palmatum* (Japanese maple) | 5 | D | 20′ | | • | • | • | • | Gracefully upright or rounded. Multitrunked. Some cultivars have reddish, bronze, or purplish foliage. *A.p.* 'Sango Kaku' has coral-colored branches. |
| *Amelanchier canadensis* (shadblow) | 5 | D | 25′ | • | • | • | • | • | Mass of white flowers in early spring, followed by purplish foliage that ages to green, and dark blue fruit in early summer. Striking gray bark shows when tree is bare. |
| *Cercis chinensis* (Chinese redbud) | 8 | D | 12′ | • | | • | • | | Shrubby tree with clusters of rose-purple flowers preceding heart-shaped leaves. Yellow fall color. Excellent in desert areas. Many other *C.* species, some much larger, adapt to particular climate areas throughout most of the country. |
| *Chamaecyparis obtusa* (Hinoki cypress) | 5 | E | 40′ | | • | | • | | Attractively asymmetrical, spreading habit. Many dwarf forms: See listing under Small Shrubs. |

| | Hardy to U.S.D.A. Zone | Deciduous/Evergreen | Height | Special Ornamental Value | Flowers | Fruit or Seed | Green Foliage | Fall Foliage | Habit/Branching Pattern |
|---|---|---|---|---|---|---|---|---|---|
| **LARGE TREES AND SHRUBS (12 feet or more) (continued)** | | | | | | | | | |
| *Cornus florida* (flowering dogwood) | 5 | D | 25' | • | • | • | • | • | Many cultivars with white, pink, or reddish flowers. *C. kousa* and *C. mas* also appropriate. Most *C.* cultivars have vivid red fall foliage and berries. |
| *Cryptomeria japonica* (Japanese cedar) | 7 | E | variable 20–90' | • | • | | | • | Species becomes huge in time. *C.j.* 'Elegans' reaches only 20'. Both have attractively shredded reddish brown bark and blue-green short needles that turn purplish brown in winter. Japanese cedar accepts heavy pruning. |
| *Diospyros kaki* (Japanese persimmon) | 7 | D | 30' | | • | • | • | • | Bare tree festooned with large orange-red fruit splendid in late autumn and early winter, after gold-to-scarlet leaves have fallen. Variety 'Hachiya' with its huge acorn-shaped fruit is especially striking. Excellent accent tree. |
| *Ginkgo biloba* (maidenhair tree) | 5 | D | 60' | | | • | • | • | Open, airy habit. Slow growing, hardy, and tough. Fan-shaped leaves are bright green, then rather suddenly pure yellow in fall. Buy male tree to avoid messy, smelly fruit. |
| *Ilex crenata* (Japanese holly) | 7 | E | 20' | | • | • | | • | Many cultivars, varying from the species in size, habit (upright or low and rounded), leaf size, shape, finish, and spininess. Female tree must have a male nearby to fruit. |
| *Koelreuteria paniculata* (golden-rain tree) | 6 | D | 20' | • | • | • | | | Slow-growing, rounded, open tree with compound leaves. Pendulous clusters of yellow summer flowers followed by papery, lanternlike seed pods. Adaptable to unusual range of soils and climates. |
| *Magnolia stellata* (star magnolia) | 6 | D | 15' | • | • | • | | • | Fragrant flowers, white, pink, or purplish, before leaves appear. Multitrunked, slow growing, shrubby. Attractive ornamental fruit. Excellent accent tree. |
| *Osmanthus fragrans* (sweet olive) | 8 | E | 12' | • | | • | • | | Heavy flowering in early spring, intermittently into fall. Neat, compact habit. |
| *Pinus thunbergiana* (Japanese black pine) | 5 | E | 20–100' | | • | • | | • | Extremely malleable species, height and shape easily controlled by pruning. Cultivars of other pines, notably of *P. sylvestris* (Scots pine) and *P. densiflora* 'Umbraculifera' (Tanyosho pine), keep small size. |
| *Pittosporum tobira* (Japanese pittosporum) | 8 | E | 12–18' | • | | • | • | | Thick, leathery leaves and, in early summer, clusters of orange-scented, creamy white flowers. |
| *Prunus cerasifera*, various cultivars (cherry plum) | 4 | D | variable 15–40' | • | • | • | • | • | Many beautiful cultivars of this and other species of flowering plum, variable in foliage and flower color and in habit. Very early flowering. Edible small fruit from some cultivars. |
| *Prunus mume* (Japanese apricot) | 7 | D | 20' | • | • | | | • | White, pink, deep red, or rose flowers appear in late winter. Long-lived tree becomes attractively gnarled with age. |
| *Prunus serrulata* (Japanese flowering cherry) | 6 | D | variable 10–30' | • | | | • | • | Many cultivars, variable in size, habit, flower tone. The hallmark of spring gardens in Japan. |
| *Sciadopitys verticillata* (Japanese umbrella pine) | 6 | E | 25–100' | • | • | | • | | Glossy needles in dense whorls. Habit is compact, symmetrically pyramidal. Growth rate very slow at first. Can be kept in container or controlled through pruning. |
| *Tsuga canadensis* (Canada hemlock) | 3 | E | 20–80' | • | • | | | | Shiny dark green needles. May be pruned as permanent hedge or screen. |

# MEDIUM TREES AND SHRUBS

Some medium-size shrubs (*Acer palmatum* 'Dissectum,' for example) are often used as focal specimens or as container plants displayed seasonally, when they are flowering, fruiting, or showing autumn color. During other seasons they are kept outside the main garden area. Most deciduous shrubs are used chiefly for their brief show of color. Even though some evergreens such as camellias have beautiful seasonal flowers, they are used largely as background, for their various textures and shades of green. Those with distinctive form and particular features, such as nandina and lily-of-the-valley shrub, are often used to great advantage as specimens, in the ground or containers. Dense, fine-textured evergreens (such as Armstrong juniper) may be shaped to echo and soften the forms of rocks among which they are planted. They may be planted in groups and shaped into low mounds to suggest rolling ranges of hills or mountains in the middle or background.

*A lily-of-the-valley shrub (*Pieris japonica*) with brilliant new growth is interplanted with a rhododendron hybrid in a woodland garden.*

| | Hardy to U.S.D.A. Zone | Deciduous/Evergreen | Height | Special Ornamental Value | Flowers | Fruit or Seed | Green Foliage | Fall Foliage | Habit/Branching Pattern |
|---|---|---|---|---|---|---|---|---|---|
| **MEDIUM TREES AND SHRUBS (4 to 11 feet)** | | | | | | | | | |
| *Acer palmatum* 'Dissectum' (laceleaf Japanese maple) | 6 | D | 3–6' | | • | • | • | • | Gracefully arching branches, form that increases in character with age. Deeply cut leaves, bright green in summer and yellow in fall, burn and curl in dry, windy areas. Other named, grafted cultivars of *A.p.* vary greatly in color, habit, size. |
| *Aucuba japonica* (Japanese aucuba) | 7 | E | 5–10' | | • | • | | • | Compact, rounded (or in deep shade, eventually open) shrub with large, waxy, serrated dark green leaves, red winter berries. Many of the named cultivars of *A.j.* are variously variegated. |
| *Camellia japonica* hybrids (common camellia) | 8 | E | variable 5–12' | • | | • | | • | Dense, rounded or upright habit. Shiny thick leaves and exquisite large flowers in the white-pink-red range, appear fall to spring depending on variety. *C. sasanqua* (sasanqua camellia) cultivars are either dense and compact or open and airy, with small leaves and small, profuse, short-lived flowers in fall or early winter. |
| *Chaenomeles* hybrids (flowering quince) | 5 | D | variable 3–8' | • | • | • | | • | Form most interesting when leafless, especially when late-fall or early-winter flowers appear before leaves. It looks best when thinned by pruning, and it lends itself to pruning for special effects. Flowers of the many named cultivars are in the white-pink-apricot-red range. |

*Left: A camellia variety blooms in early spring. Throughout the year its glossy foliage enhances the garden. In the background, notice the sheared hedge of Kurume azalea.*

*Opposite: The texture of elegantly mounded David viburnum contrasts with that of the Japanese holly 'Convexa' that flanks it. Blossoms of the viburnum will be followed by beautiful metallic blue berries.*

| | Hardy to U.S.D.A. Zone | Deciduous/Evergreen | Height | Special Ornamental Value | Flowers | Fruit or Seed | Green Foliage | Fall Foliage | Habit/Branching Pattern |
|---|---|---|---|---|---|---|---|---|---|
| **MEDIUM TREES AND SHRUBS (4 to 11 feet) (continued)** | | | | | | | | | |
| *Forsythia × intermedia* (border forsythia) | 5 | D | 8–10′ | • | | • | | • | Graceful fountain form requiring annual thinning. Yellow flowers cover bare branches in late winter or early spring, followed by clear green foliage. |
| *Juniperus chinensis* 'Armstrongii' (Armstrong juniper) | 4 | E | 4′ | | • | • | | • | Compact, upright habit, bluish green foliage. This juniper is tough, adaptable, and malleable. |
| *Mahonia bealei* (leatherleaf mahonia) | 7 | E | 7′ | • | • | • | | • | Interesting upright, open habit and attractive foliage pattern. Handsome whorls of large, stiff, symmetrical compound leaves; fragrant small yellow late-spring flowers followed by dark, grapelike berries. |
| *Nandina domestica* (heavenly bamboo) | 7 | E | 8′ | | • | • | • | • | Not bamboo but a woody shrub with multiple trunks and loose whorls of feathery, rather bamboolike foliage. Deep-red new growth, scarlet autumn foliage, and scarlet berries together with the graceful habit make this a very popular shrub in Japan. Dwarf cultivars add more possibilities in the garden. |
| *Pieris japonica* (lily-of-the-valley shrub) | 6 | E | 9′ | • | | • | | • | Narrow, glossy leaves in dense tiers, pendulous clusters of white spring flowers, and year-round overall sightliness. Well placed among azaleas and ferns. The many *P.* cultivars include dwarf and variegated forms. |
| *Rhododendron* Exbury hybrids (Exbury hybrid azaleas) | 6 | D | 4–8′ | • | | • | • | • | Huge array of cultivars in wide range of colors: white-yellow-pink-orange-red range. Large clusters of flowers appear at branch tips in late spring. Other deciduous azaleas suited to particular climate areas can be just as effective in the garden. |

## MINIATURE OR SMALL, MOUNDING SHRUBS

Small shrubs frequently echo the shapes of rocks they are planted among or make a low background (especially useful when a viewing point is above them) for focal features such as stones or lanterns. Most are slow growing. Most listed here lend themselves to shearing or other shaping, because of their compactness and density. An exception in this list is the David viburnum, which naturally forms a compact mound but whose large, veined leaves, with their splendid sculptural quality, do not lend themselves at all to shearing.

| | Hardy to U.S.D.A. Zone | Deciduous/Evergreen | Height | Special Ornamental Value | Flowers | Fruit or Seed | Green Foliage | Fall Foliage | Habit/Branching Pattern |
|---|---|---|---|---|---|---|---|---|---|
| **MINIATURE OR SMALL, MOUNDING SHRUBS (to 3 feet)** | | | | | | | | | |
| *Buxus microphylla* (littleleaf box) | 6 | E | 3′ | | | • | • | | Compact, fine-textured shrub. The named cultivars differ from the species in size, habit, or leaf color and shape. |
| *Chamaecyparis obtusa* 'Nana' (dwarf Hinoki cypress) | 4 | E | 2′ | | | • | • | | A roundish or rather flat dwarf that holds its dull green, scalelike foliage in small, fanlike tufts, creating a splendid form with striking texture. Extremely slow growing, it and other cultivars vary in size, color, and habit. |
| *Daphne cneorum* (garland flower) | 5 | E | 6″ | | • | • | • | | Small, narrow evergreen leaves, mounding habit, and late-spring flowers at branch tips, rosy purple and strongly fragrant. It thrives in moist limestone or peaty soils. |
| *Hebe buxifolia* (boxleaf hebe) | 7 | E | 3′ | | • | • | • | | Compact, rounded shrub requiring little pruning to look sheared. It is densely covered by tiny leaves and, in summer, white flowers that attract bees. |
| *Juniperus chinensis* 'Blue Vase' (Texas star juniper) | 4 | E | 3′ | • | | • | • | | Compact, dense shrub, broad as it is high, with bluish, spiny foliage. |
| *Pinus mugo* 'Compacta' (compact mugo pine) | 3 | E | 3′ | | | • | • | | Roundish, squat miniature with dense growth, short needles. It fares rather poorly in hot, dry areas. |
| *Rhododendron* Kurume hybrids (Kurume hybrid azaleas) | 6 | E | 3′ | | • | • | • | | Large group of azalea hybrids, compact and variable in habit, from roundish mounds to higher, looser plants. In spring, they are completely covered by blossoms. Colors vary from shades of dark red to pink and white. |
| *Spiraea* × *bumalda* 'Anthony Waterer' (dwarf red spiraea) | 6 | D | 2′ | | • | • | • | | Rounded, dense habit and heavy, then intermittent, summer flowers: large, flat clusters of tiny red blossoms. Spring foliage is often pink tinged. |
| *Thuja occidentalis* 'Globosa' (globe or Tom Thumb arborvitae) | 4 | E | 2–3′ | | | • | • | | Compact, rounded shrub, with dense sprays of gray-green, scalelike foliage. |
| *Viburnum davidii* (David viburnum) | 7 | E | 2–3′ | • | | • | • | | Striking, compact, symmetrical miniature with mounding, slightly spreading habit. Glossy, sculpted leaves with parallel veins together with bunches of turquoise berries. |

*Right: This water lily 'Sultan' provides a long summer season of splendid blossoms. Opposite: Chinese wisteria with its gnarled trunk overhangs Kurume azalea 'Hinodegiri' and a ground cover of ajuga. The soft-textured, pendulous tree in the background is a deodar cedar.*

## WATER AND WATER'S-EDGE PLANTS

Nothing next to a dry stream or pond suggests water more persuasively than a water's-edge plant and, in or around a real water feature, nothing else provides such a graceful, natural touch, obscuring the sharp line between water and shore and creating a soft transition. Water's-edge plants look best in clumps or in patches. Their verticality makes a pleasing contrast to the plane of the water or suggested water, and accentuates their reflections.

| | Hardy to U.S.D.A. Zone | Deciduous/Evergreen | Height | Special Ornamental Value | Flowers | Fruit or Seed | Green Foliage | Fall Foliage | Habit/Branching Pattern |
|---|---|---|---|---|---|---|---|---|---|
| **WATER AND WATER'S-EDGE PLANTS** | | | | | | | | | |
| *Acorus gramineus* (sweet flag) | 6 | E | 12–18″ | | • | | • | | Quarter-inch-wide leaves forming sculptural tufts. One cultivar has white-striped leaves. *A.g.* thrives at a pond's edge or in a container. |
| *Cyperus isocladus* (*C. papyrus* 'Nanus') (dwarf papyrus) | 10* | E | 18″ | • | • | | • | | *Hardy indoor-outdoor plant in any climate zone. Foliage is actually sheaths around stems that persist the year around where protected from frost. Except in frost-free areas, it is best planted in pots, submerged, then taken indoors as a houseplant during the cold season. |
| *Iris Kaempferi* (Japanese iris) | 5 | D | 2′ | • | • | | • | | Long, slender leaves on branched, upright stems, topped by huge, flat blossoms in white-purple-blue-pink range, often with contrasting petal edges. Plant at water's edge or in half-submerged seasonal containers. |
| *Nelumbo nucifera* (sacred lotus) | * | D | 3–7′ | • | • | • | • | | *Hardy anywhere submerged rhizomes can't freeze. Dramatically large, beautiful 1- to 2-foot leaves, held high above water alongside showy pink summer flowers (some cultivars have white or rose, single or double ones). Appropriate only for large ponds. *N.n.* flowers better if planted in pond bottoms, but invasiveness makes submerged containers preferable where planting must be held in check. |
| *Nymphaea* species and hybrids (water lily) | 3–10* | D | ** | • | • | | | | *Tender tropicals can be planted anywhere in containers and stored over winter in damp sand. **Leaves of most cultivars lie on or close to water; blossoms of some, to 6 inches above water. Round padlike leaves and flowers in white-yellow-pink-red range; tropicals, in the blue, purple, and blue-green range. |

*Above left: Soft plumes of astilbe are favorite color accents in the gardens of Japan. Japanese iris grow with the astilbe beside the stream.*
*Above right: A white form of Japanese anemone displays delicate stems and fall blossoms.*

## PERENNIALS

Used sparingly in traditional Japanese gardens as accents, perennials make seasonal color and some reinforce the emotional qualities of a season (for example, bronze-toned chrysanthemums conjure up the sweet sadness of autumn). Most—but balloon flower and aster are exceptions here—bloom for only a short time. Many, such as daylily and hosta, make a handsome large-scale ground cover for spacious gardens. Hellebore is notable not just because it flowers in winter, but also because, in partial shade, its handsome evergreen foliage makes it a perfect accompaniment to a rock, lantern, or basin.

The common snowdrop is included as a perennial in this chart. The snowdrop, like all early season bulbs, provides a brief (and, in this case, appropriately restrained) display of blossoms. Other bulbs which are suitable (including plants with rhizomes, corms, and tubers) include *Convallaria majalis* (lily of the valley), which makes a spring and summer cover of lush green; crocus; autumn crocus

(*Colchicum*); cyclamen; *Erythronium* (trout lily); *Narcissus* (preferably the small flowered varieties which will naturalize); wood hyacinth (*Hyacinthus*); and snowflake (*Leucojum*). Trillium and daylily, both listed in the chart, are often categorized as bulbs. A single bulb species of a uniform color, planted in a clump, a scattering of clumps (as in a woodland setting or under high, open shrubs), or in drifts, makes a suitably subdued display. A drawback of bulbs in a Japanese garden is the period of unsightliness when the leaves are fading but must not be removed as they are making food for the next year's blooms.

Because of their intense colors and long seasons of bloom, commercially popular annuals are generally unsuited to the spirit of a Japanese garden. One notable exception is *Primula malacoides* (fairy primrose), which, if planted in only one color (either white or pale lavender), can add magic to a woodland spot with its airy tiers of small blossoms above low whorls of foliage.

| | Hardy to U.S.D.A. Zone | Deciduous/Evergreen | Height | Special Ornamental Value | Flowers | Fruit or Seed | Green Foliage | Fall Foliage | Habit/Branching Pattern |
|---|---|---|---|---|---|---|---|---|---|
| **PERENNIALS** | | | | | | | | | |
| *Anemone × hybrida* (*A. japonica*) (Japanese anemone) | 6 | D | 2–5′ | • | • | | • | | Gracefully branching upright form, lobed leaves, and single or double rose-pink flowers. Inherently beautiful, and especially valuable for flowering from late summer until frost. |
| *Arisaema triphyllum* (jack-in-the-pulpit) | 5 | D | 1–2′ | • | • | • | • | | Attractive upright habit. Beautiful purple-white-green spring blossom and brilliant red autumn berries give this plant a long season of interest. |
| *Aster × Frikartii* 'Wonder of Stafa' | 5 | D | 2′ | • | • | | • | | Upright, open habit, handsome fuzzy leaves, and fragrant lavender-blue flowers through summer and fall. |
| *Astilbe* hybrids (false spiraea) | 4 | D | 18″–4′ | • | • | | • | | Airy, tapering masses of tiny pink, red, or white flowers, late spring to midsummer, atop handsome lobed foliage. |
| *Chrysanthemum × morifolium* hybrids (florist's chrysanthemum) | 4 | D | 2–5′ | • | • | | • | | Upright or mounding habit unless trained otherwise, lobed dark green leaves, and medium to large blossoms variable in size, form, and color. |
| *Galanthus nivalis* (common snowdrop) | 4 | D | 1′ | • | • | | • | | Bulbous plant that naturalizes in cold-climate woodland conditions. Nodding green-tipped white flowers, often first of the season, appearing sometimes out of snow, bloom above arching straplike leaves. |
| *Helleborus niger* (Christmas rose) | 4 | E | 1–1½′ | • | • | | • | | Graceful upright habit, glossy dark green compound leaves, and splendid greenish white flowers aging to purple. Other species begin blooming later; some thrive in warm or dry climates. |
| *Hemerocallis fulva* (tawny daylily) | 3 | D | 2–4′ | • | • | | • | | A summer-blooming species, less showy (and more appropriate to Japanese gardens) than many of the myriad *H.* hybrids. Arching, straplike leaves create pleasing texture and mass, and orange-red flowers are borne continuously for several weeks in midsummer. Some hybrids and some other species are evergreen. |
| *Hosta ventricosa* (*H. caerulea*) (blue plantain lily) | 3 | D | 3′ | • | • | | • | | Splendid clumps of broad, glossy leaves, rich green and heavily ribbed, above which violet flowers are borne on airy spires in mid- or late summer. |
| *Paeonia* species and hybrids (herbaceous peony) | 5 | D | 2–4′ | • | • | | • | | Upright habit and shiny divided leaves, above which superb large, often-fragrant flowers appear in mid- to late spring. Colors are in the white-cream-yellow-pink-red tones. Narrow-petaled types are typically Japanese. *P. suffruticosa* (Japanese tree peony) is a medium-height deciduous shrub with large, elegant flowers—a Japanese favorite. |
| *Platycodon grandiflorus* (balloon flower) | 3 | D | 2–3′ | • | • | | • | | Compact clumps of erect, branching stems with narrow blue-green leaves, topped throughout summer with globular buds ("balloons") and starlike single or double, Wedgwood-blue flowers. Other forms of *P.g.* and other *P.* species differ in color (white, soft pink, rose-lilac) and size. |
| *Trillium erectum* (purple trillium) | 3 | D | 2′ | • | • | • | • | | Clumps of upright individual stems, each bearing a whorl of three ribbed leaves beneath a single, three-petaled white flower. April to June, followed by blue-black berries. Other *T.* species adapt better in hotter or drier climates. |

| | Hardy to U.S.D.A. Zone | Deciduous/Evergreen | Height | Special Ornamental Value | Flowers | Fruit or Seed | Green Foliage | Fall Foliage | Habit/Branching Pattern |
|---|---|---|---|---|---|---|---|---|---|
| **VINES** | | | | | | | | | |
| *Clematis armandii* (evergreen clematis) | 7 | E | 15–20' | • | • | • | | • | Incomparable texture created by masses of creased, downward-pointing, glossy deep-green leaflets. Fragrant pure white flowers appear for a few weeks in spring. |
| *Hydrangea anomala petiolaris* (climbing hydrangea) | 5 | D | 30–75' | • | | • | | | Large-scale, shrubby vine that climbs aggressively, attaching to nearly any surface; damaging to wood. In midsummer, large flat heads of white flowers glisten against a backdrop of glossy, bright green foliage. |
| *Ipomoea alba* (moonflower) | * | D | 10–30' | • | | • | | | *Best grown as an annual where winters are too severe for it. Large white flowers, fully open only at night, strongly fragrant: midsummer until frost. Spade-shaped leaves are highly ornamental. |
| *Parthenocissus tricuspidata* (Boston ivy) | 5 | D | 60' | | | • | • | • | Three-lobed, glossy, rich green leaves until fall, when they turn fiery scarlet. The vine attaches firmly and flat against most surfaces. |
| *Wisteria floribunda* (Japanese wisteria) | 5 | D | variable | • | • | • | | • | Can be trained as small tree or shrub as well as vine. Old stems are attractively gnarled and massive. Species bears delicate, pendulous 18-inch clusters of fragrant, violet or blue-violet flowers in spring. Other cultivars of *W.f.* have white, blue, purple, or lavender flowers in racemes up to 3' long. *W. sinensis* (Chinese wisteria) has shorter racemes of more showy flowers. |

## VINES

On fences and walls, especially those with peaked roofs running their length, flowering vines are a great asset, softening sharp lines and, if they are evergreen, creating a permanent background for other plantings. Arbors or trellises are perfect for evergreen clematis and for wisteria. Hydrangea and Boston ivy make a dense wall cover with distinctive texture; the latter is useful for its display of bright fall color.

## FERNS

Hallmarks of Japanese gardens, ferns of almost any species conjure up a spirit of primeval woodland and fecundity. At the bases of mossy rocks or growing on them, next to water, alone, or with shrubs or perennials, ferns add immensely to the spirit of a Japanese garden. Virtually any fern that thrives and is available in your region will be harmonious with the spirit of a Japanese garden. Even tree ferns are sometimes used to great effect, though their scale and tropical look disqualify them from most small gardens and gardens whose plants are from the temperate zones.

## BAMBOOS AND OTHER GRASSES

Another hallmark of the Japanese garden, bamboo lends an airy grace to whatever setting in which it is used. From the giant timber bamboos (not listed here because of their scale) to the dwarf forms, bamboos and other tall grasses have a range of garden uses. They add verticality and their litheness makes them a constantly moving part of even a courtyard garden. They cast rippling shadows on the ground and vertical surfaces. Smaller forms can be trimmed into compact hedges and into mounds that suggest rocks, or can be left in their naturally dense form as small shrublike plants used, for example, to edge a path. Groves or clumps of the bigger varieties make beautiful features, or screens. Most bamboos make excellent container plants. Clumping bamboos do spread, but very slowly; running bamboos spread rapidly and you must take great care to contain them with a shield of impermeable, solid material sunk between 18 and 24 inches into the ground all around them. Their tendency to take over wherever planted cannot be overemphasized.

*Opposite left: Chinese wisteria hangs over a lush bed of sword fern, a close relative of the Boston fern. Note the weathered wood support used to prop the blossom-heavy wisteria bough. Opposite right: Young specimens of* Sphaeropteris cooperi, *the Australian tree fern, lend a lush, tropical feeling to this moist garden area. Their texture contrasts interestingly with other foliage in the area. Like most ferns, they look at home among stones.*

| | Hardy to U.S.D.A. Zone | Deciduous/Evergreen | Height | Special Ornamental Value | Flowers | Fruit or Seed | Green Foliage | Fall Foliage | Habit/Branching Pattern |
|---|---|---|---|---|---|---|---|---|---|
| **FERNS** | | | | | | | | | |
| *Adiantum pedatum* (American maidenhair fern) | 4 | D | 1–2′ | | | • | • | • | Perhaps the daintiest, most airy fern, with wirelike near-black stems and bright green leaflets that seem to float. Fingerlike branches of fronds create nearly horizontal fans. Autumn color ranges from yellow to muted gold. |
| *Athyrium filix-femina* (lady fern) | 3 | E/D* | 1½–3′ | | | • | | • | *Evergreen or semievergreen in mild areas, deciduous elsewhere. Vaselike form, with very finely cut, lacy yellow-green fronds. Several cultivars are available. |
| *Cyrtomium falcatum* (Japanese holly fern) | 10* | E | 1–3′ | | | • | | • | *Container culture permits indoor-outdoor use in colder climates. Bold-textured fern with open form and large, shapely leaflets that remain glossy dark green throughout the year. |
| *Polypodium virginianum* (rock polypody, American wall fern) | 5 | E | 10″ | | | • | | • | Fern found in the wild on rocks and cliffs. Fronds are deeply divided. With mosses and lichens, creates wonderfully naturalistic effects on garden rocks. |
| *Polystichum acrostichoides* (Christmas fern) | 4 | E | 2′ | | | • | | • | Spreading; similar in appearance to popular houseplant Boston fern. Some forms are lacy textured. |

*Left: Black bamboo adds verticality and softness to an area paved with Scotch moss and planted with a young specimen of sword fern.*
*Right: A very different feeling is achieved with this yellow grove bamboo by hand-stripping the lower stems of foliage. The effect is that of a dense, miniature forest grove.*

| | Hardy to U.S.D.A. Zone | Deciduous/Evergreen | Height | Special Ornamental Value | Flowers | Fruit or Seed | Green Foliage | Fall Foliage | Habit/Branching Pattern |
|---|---|---|---|---|---|---|---|---|---|
| **BAMBOOS AND OTHER GRASSES** | | | | | | | | | |
| *Arundinaria pygmaea (Sasa pygmaea)* (pygmy bamboo) | 7 | E | 12–18″ | | | • | | • | An aggressive running bamboo with bright green foliage and low, bushy habit. It can be used as ground cover and mowed periodically. A variegated form is often available. |
| *Arundinaria simonii* (Simon bamboo) | 7 | E | 10–25′ | | | • | | • | Gracefully vertical, moderately aggressive running bamboo, suitable as screen. There is a variegated form. |
| *Bambusa glaucescens* 'Fern Leaf' *(B. distacha)* (fernleaf hedge bamboo) | 8 | E | 6–20′ | | | • | | • | Clumping, with fountainlike habit. Its ferny look is created by closely spaced leaves and thin, reedy stems. |
| *Bambusa glaucesens* 'Golden Goddess' (golden goddess bamboo) | 8 | E | 6–10′ | | | • | | • | Clumping, with dense, arching habit. |
| *Pennisetum setaceum* (fountain grass) | 7* | D | 2–4′ | • | | • | | • | *In coldest areas, lift plants, or treat as annuals, starting from seed indoors, then transplanting out. Fountain-shaped clumps of slender, arching leaves and curving, dense bristly flower and seed heads. Pink, red, rose, and purple forms are sometimes available. |
| *Phyllostachys aureosulcata* (yellow-groove bamboo) | 7 | E | 12–30′ | | | • | | • | A running bamboo with dense, vertical habit. Young stems have yellow-green grooves. This is the hardiest bamboo, excellent as screen or contained specimen. |
| *Phyllostachys nigra* (black bamboo) | 7 | E | 4–15′ | | | • | | • | A running bamboo with arching, open habit. This is perhaps the most striking bamboo, with its bright green leaves and stems speckled when young, then solid black. |
| *Sasa veitchii* (kuma bamboo grass) | 8 | E | 2–4′ | | | • | • | • | A diminutive running bamboo with large, bright green leaves. In late fall and winter, leaves have precisely delineated, straw-colored edges, creating a subtle effect. |
| *Shibataea kumasaca* | 8 | E | 2–6′ | | | • | | • | A slow-spreading runner, forming low, dense clumps. |
| *Sinarundinaria nitida* | 7 | E | 2–6′ | | | • | | • | Clumping, with airy, arching habit and deep purple stems. |

# GROUND COVERS

In an area large enough, even sizeable shrubs can make a ground cover. Listed here are low shrubs (whose scale suits most home gardens), fine-textured moss substitutes, and perennial plants of various textures. Moss—club moss as well as real moss—is preferred in Japan wherever its scale suits the design and conditions allow it to flourish. In this country, it grows best in the wet, mild areas of the Pacific Northwest but hardly ever in hot, arid areas. Therefore substitutes have been suggested. Another traditional Japanese ground cover is lawn grass, so you should not hesitate to use it where appropriate.

All ground covers listed here are evergreen, with the exception of Korean grass, which browns but keeps its form through winter. Almost all ground covers require frequent cleaning, especially the tiny, fine-textured ones, in order to keep them exposed to sun and air. The shrubby ones and perennials require less maintenance but are harder to clean, because the work must be done by hand. Some very dense covers discourage weeds, while others require careful, frequent weeding.

| | Hardy to U.S.D.A. Zone | Deciduous/Evergreen | Height | Special Ornamental Value | Flowers | Fruit or Seed | Green Foliage | Fall Foliage | Habit/Branching Pattern |
|---|---|---|---|---|---|---|---|---|---|
| **GROUND COVERS: SHRUBS** | | | | | | | | | |
| *Abelia × grandiflora* 'Prostrata' (prostrate glossy abelia) | 6 | E* | 1–2′ | • | | • | | | *Evergreen or semideciduous. Creeping habit, shiny small leaves, and a sprinkling of small pinkish white, slightly fragrant flowers in summer and early fall. |
| *Arctostaphylos uva-ursi* (bearberry) | 2 | E | 3–5″ | • | • | • | • | | Prostrate shrub with small, shiny, oval leaves, clusters of small white flowers at branch tips in late spring or early summer, followed by red berries. Some or all leaves turn red during winter. |
| *Juniperus horizontalis* 'Wiltonii' (blue carpet juniper) | 3 | E | 3–4″ | | • | • | • | | The lowest juniper, which forms a dense, uniform mat. Intensely gray-blue foliage turns bluish purple in winter. |
| *Pachysandra terminalis* (Japanese spurge) | 5 | E | 6–12″ | • | • | • | | • | Upright plants forming uniformly dense patches; can be invasive if not contained. Attractive lustrous dark green leaves in round clusters at stem ends. In late spring, small erect spikes of white flowers appear, followed in fall by white berries. Foliage looks best when *P.t.* is grown in full to half shade. |
| *Sarcococca hookeriana humilis* (small Himalayan sweet box) | 6 | E | 1–3′ | | • | • | | • | Prostrate branches clothed densely in dark, shiny leaves. Early-spring flowers are inconspicuous but very fragrant. They are followed by glossy dark berries. *S.h.h.* accepts even deep shade. |
| **GROUND COVERS: MOSSLIKE PLANTS** | | | | | | | | | |
| *Mentha requienii* (jewel mint of Corsica) | 7 | E* | ½″ | • | | • | | • | *Dies back and goes dormant in cold areas. Minuscule leaves that give off strong peppermint scent when crushed, and mid- to late-summer tiny lavender flowers. |
| *Sagina subulata* (Irish moss and Scotch moss) | 5 | E | ¼″* | • | | • | | • | *Flower stems to 4 inches. Dense enough to make a solid, mounding mass between stepping stones or in an open area. Tiny individual white flowers appear in midsummer. The form called Irish moss is rich dark green; Scotch moss is yellowish green. Two quite similar plants with the same common names and equal value in the Japanese garden are varieties of *Arenaria verna*. |

*A drift of pachysandra makes a neatly contained evergreen ground cover and a graceful form, which extends outward from the taller plantings around the simple garden pavilion. A flowering cherry 'Shogetsu' blooms in the foreground.*

| | Hardy to U.S.D.A. Zone | Deciduous/Evergreen | Height | Special Ornamental Value | Flowers | Fruit or Seed | Green Foliage | Fall Foliage | Habit/Branching Pattern |
|---|---|---|---|---|---|---|---|---|---|
| **GROUND COVERS: MOSSLIKE PLANTS (continued)** | | | | | | | | | |
| *Soleirolia soleirolii* (baby's tears) | 10 | E | 1–3″ | | • | | • | | Fine-textured, lush creeping plant with tiny, delicate, medium- or golden-green leaves on thin stems. It thrives in light to medium shade. |
| *Thymus praecox arcticus* (*T. serpyllum*) (creeping thyme) | 4 | E | 1–3″ | • | • | | • | | Tiny upright branches with ¼-inch, intensely aromatic leaves and, late spring to early fall, white or pale violet flowers. This and other sun-loving thymes are adaptable to a wide range of climates. |
| *Zoysia tenuifolia* (Korean grass) | 10 | D* | 3–5″ | | • | | • | | *Blades turn brown in winter but maintain the form of the plant. An exceptionally tough, fine-textured grass that creates an attractively irregular, mounding surface. |
| **GROUND COVERS: PERENNIALS** | | | | | | | | | |
| *Asarum caudatum* (wild ginger) | 5 | E | 7–10″ | | • | | • | | In rich, shaded soil forms a lush, bold-textured cover of glossy heart-shaped leaves. Inconspicuous flowers at plant bases are attractively curious. |
| *Epimedium grandiflorum* (bishop's hat) | 3 | * | 9–12″ | • | • | • | • | | *Semievergreen or evergreen. Airy plant with wiry stems. Red to violet to white flowers with spurred, hatlike form are borne on upright spikes, late spring or early summer. Other *E.* and related *Vancouveria* species are useful in woodland conditions. |
| *Galax urceolata* (*G. aphylla*) (wandflower) | 4 | E | 6″* | • | • | | • | • | *Leaves held up to 6 inches high, flowers spikes to 18 inches. Basal rosettes of splendid shiny, nearly round leaves that turn bronzy in fall and winter; slender spikes of tiny white flowers in midsummer. |
| *Iberis sempervirens* (edging candytuft) | 4 | E | 6–12″ | • | • | | • | | Compact, tiny-leaved plants forming neat, dark green mats with roundish heads of white flowers in late spring. Various named cultivars differ in size and habit. |
| *Ophiopogon japonicus* (mondo grass) | 7 | E | 6–10″ | • | • | • | • | | Narrow, linear, arching dark green leaves forming turf with beautiful grasslike texture. In summer, dense tapering spikes of small lavender flowers followed by blue berries. Other species of *O.* and closely related *Liriope* (lily turf) are useful in Japanese gardens. |

## PRUNING AND SPECIAL MAINTENANCE

With some variation, the most basic horticultural techniques are universal. Using the same materials and tools that you would use in any garden, you can plant, feed, water, weed, and clean your garden. A Japanese garden, by its very nature, demands meticulous care. Weeds, pests, and diseases don't distinguish a Japanese-style garden from any other, so use the same control methods that you would use in any garden. The basics of horticulture need no explanation here, but there are a few principles and special techniques that you should understand, especially for pruning (here the term includes pinching, shearing, and clipping) but also for other methods of shaping and controlling trees and some shrubs. Some Japanese gardening techniques, such as wrapping tender plants for winter protection, are more picturesque and difficult than they are practical in the context of a residential American garden, and are omitted here.

### Pruning

Two very important, closely related, and often overlapping purposes of pruning (and pinching back, shearing, and clipping) are those of controlling growth and shaping. A third is that of admitting light to the lower branches and plantings beneath pruned plants.

For all three purposes, the season for pruning is important. Evergreens should be pruned or pinched in late spring and again at the end of summer. Deciduous trees may be pinched or clipped in any season, but actual pruning (that is, the cutting of branches) is best done in fall. Pruning to remove diseased parts of any plant should be done immediately when the problem is discovered, in any season. Fruit trees in Japanese gardens are pruned according to the universal calendar for the care of fruit trees.

All forms of pruning should be restrained when trees and shrubs grow under very stressful conditions, such as in salty or polluted air or in very poor or shallow soil. Too little foliage might remain to produce food for the plants.

**Pruning to control height** A Japanese garden maker designs a garden with an appropriate ultimate size in mind for every tree, hedge, and shrub. Americans, however, tend to let shrubs and trees grow indefinitely, without any concept of what would be considered too large.

*Above left: Irish moss (*Selaginella kraussiana 'Brownii'*) is a striking ground cover and provides a contrast to the cone-shaped dwarf white spruce (*Picea glauca 'Conica'*) specimens and other evergreens.*
*Above right: The clump of mondo grass complements the juniper and iris and makes a dramatic and simple form among gravel and stones. It can also serve well as a ground cover.*

Many varieties of
flowering quince
provide an elegant,
open, angular form, if
growth is thinned and
natural habit is
accentuated by
pruning. Here the
seasonal pruning
is just underway.

On the right common
boxwood is pruned to
exaggerate its regular,
rounded shape that
complements the stone
grouping by echoing
the roundness of the
stone on the left. A less
controlled Japanese
boxwood 'Green
Beauty' and a
compact form of
heavenly bamboo
nestle into the center,
and a pleasing
contrast is provided
on the left by fortnight
lily, an evergreen
relative of irises.

This Japanese black
pine has been shaped
not only through
pruning. In a
traditional Japanese
manner, bamboo
braces, attached to the
branches with rope,
encourage the
branches to spread in
a particular way that
suggests the natural
habit of an old, wind-
blown pine. Braces
will be removed when
the effect has been
achieved.

The Japanese make gardens in which trees and large shrubs provide just the right degree of enclosure and just the right mass according to the nature of each tree or shrub and its relation to the house, to another garden feature (such as a stone with which it forms a composition), or to the rest of the garden—in each case, a matter of proportion. In small gardens, it is particularly important to keep every plant strictly within the limits of its appropriate ultimate size. Most basic design principles depend at least in part on the size of the plants with which you are working.

It is sensible to use a slow-growing species whose size can usually be controlled by pruning. But even a well-chosen plant may eventually insist on growing out of bounds. If proper scale can no longer be maintained by pruning, the plant must be replaced.

**Pruning to shape**   In pruning a plant to shape it, you essentially accentuate or exaggerate its natural form. Even topiary domes or mounds are shaped out of shrubs that are naturally of a rounded or mounding habit. Sometimes their shapes echo or blend with the shapes of nearby stones. A pine is often shaped to a layered, opened up, spreading exaggeration of its natural shape.

Occasionally a shrub or tree is pruned without regard for its natural form, toward soft or hard-edged angles. Such abstraction of form may balance the wild forms of adjacent stones and vegetation or create a transition between the symmetry of the house and the asymmetry of the garden.

Pruning a dense shrub or tree to shape may actually constitute shearing, if the foliage is very fine and the desired effect is smoothness. If foliage is coarse enough to look butchered when sheared, or if a slightly more natural look is desired, clipping is called for, cutting the individual tips will produce the desired form, but the plant will have a looser, less-controlled texture.

Most trees and large shrubs, under ordinary conditions, grow more or less straight up. In Japanese gardens, differences in habit are valued, so that some trees and shrubs grow upward but others are pruned to grow in curves or at slight angles. If the garden setting suggests a wind-swept mountain or seaside promontory, all trees may be shaped so that

they bend in the same direction. In any case, bending adds grace and a feeling of great age to the plantings.

**Pruning to open up**   Pruning to alter shape or to control growth may also be a way to open up the plant. For example, a basic pruning practice is to remove vertical growth from an essentially layered form such as that of a pine. The shaping and limiting in height also allows light through to the lower branches. Japanese prune extensively to admit light— and air—to the lower branches and inner areas of trees and the plants beneath. Healthier, less disease-prone plants will result from this practice. The lower branches remain alive, so that the desired shape of the tree is maintained. This kind of pruning must be done constantly to maintain the effect.

*An exceptionally elegant old Tanyosho pine, dwarfed by periodic pinching of buds, exhibits a layered habit that accentuates the inherent form of the tree. Notice how graceful and natural this tree appears; conversely a tree that is insensitively poodled into heavy, dense tufts would hardly resemble the natural form of the species.*

Generally, the method is to thin branches, first by removing any whose direction of growth is at odds with the desired shape, and then by removing those that crowd, cross, or directly overshadow other branches. The remaining branches are staggered vertically.

Some species which have naturally tiered branches, such as *Podocarpus macrophyllus* (yew podocarpus), are pruned so that foliage and branchlets are removed from the center of the tree and from between the tiers to open the tree both laterally and vertically. The purpose of this style of pruning is aesthetic as well as practical: It shapes as well as opens up.

Pines may be kept open, and their growth controlled by bud pinching. In spring, about two thirds of each new bud is pinched off. At the end of summer, the needles on last year's growth are removed, along with some needles from the new growth. Also, if three buds formed where the bud was pinched, the middle one is pinched off. This pinching process is invaluable, but needle plucking, though it makes the tree airier, is not practical for most American home gardeners because it is so time consuming.

### Other Shaping Methods

Pruning is not the only way to shape trees. By tying on weights near the ends of supple (not brittle) branches, you can train them to arch. Branches may also be pulled down with rope (rather than wire, which cuts into and will damage the branch) and held down to stakes in the ground. When the arch is clearly permanent, remove the weights or ropes.

When long, arching branches become too heavy with age and are liable to be broken by snow and ice, or by wind, the Japanese bolster them in various ways. A common method is the use of a T-shaped support. For a more natural appearance, the wood of the support should be weathered, and stained or weathered rope may be used as reinforcement.

Vines, particularly heavy, woody ones such as wisteria, also need a sturdy framework for support. Heavy bamboo looks quite appropriate, but heavy-duty commercial trellises will do as well. In the vine chart, note the caution against using climbing hydrangea on wooden surfaces, such as the exterior of a house. Other vines can be attached to walls, arbors, and fences, and buildings in the same way they are attached in occidental gardens.

### Plant Replacement

In Japan a standard form of garden maintenance is plant replacement. Sick, dying, malformed, or irremediably overgrown plants are torn out and replaced by new ones. Because the plan of a Japanese garden calls for a given scale, as discussed early in this chapter, any plant that cannot be kept to scale through pruning is replaced. So is any plant that is past its prime. The Japanese garden exists to embody nature in an ideal state, and anything detracting from that ideal must be altered.

This practice might at first seem drastic to American gardeners. Besides, many gardeners pride themselves on their success in keeping an aging plant going, or reviving an ailing one. But a Japanese garden isn't a laboratory. The Japanese value the preservation of the original garden design and the healthy freshness of the garden above any attachment to a plant, even an old tree, if it is declining or can no longer be kept pruned to proper scale.

## A NOTE ABOUT BONSAI

Bonsai, the artfully dwarfed and shaped container plants created by the Japanese and so widely admired in the United States, are not a traditional component of the garden. The Japanese grow them in a special area outdoors, apart from the garden proper. From time to time, as a prized bonsai comes into leaf, bloom, fruit, or fall color, it is moved into a living area—but if indoors, only into a cool room, and for only a few hours at a time. Some Japanese do display bonsai in the garden, along with other container plants that are there either temporarily or permanently.

Be extremely careful, if you use bonsai in the garden, temporarily or permanently, that you protect these works of art that have taken so much skill and so many years to create. Give them growing conditions appropriate to the same species growing in the ground. But bear in mind how quickly the soil can dry out in wind or heat, and what lasting damage extreme cold might also do to the shallow, contained roots. Usually less full midday and afternoon sun than the species prefers when growing in the ground is best.

Be mindful of the fact that a miniature plant, certainly a contained one, may destroy the very effect in the courtyard garden that is most desired.

*Below left: Grown in a lath-protected area and watered through drip irrigation to ensure that soil in the shallow containers doesn't dry out, these fine old bonsai thrive. Shown are a miniature grove of Chinese pistache, above, and a grove of Japanese maple. Below right: This bonsai Japanese maple contrasts boldly with the rustic stucco wall against which it is placed.*

# Profile of a Japanese Garden

*When the owners of the garden featured in this chapter purchased their home, they immediately set about creating a Japanese-style garden that would be harmonious with the house and entirely visible from indoors.*

They built a garden that, in its details, unity with the house, and evocation of nature, is thoroughly Japanese, yet has been thoughtfully adapted to its American setting and their needs.

Aside from its overall purpose of providing a serene sanctuary where nature may be contemplated, the garden serves more particular purposes. It creates an appropriate setting for a collection of exceptionally fine old Japanese garden ornaments, incorporates a small but choice collection of ancient Japanese trees, and functions as the perfect visual extension of indoor living space. Instead of demanding attention in the manner of a grand showplace, the garden exists quietly, inviting the discerning eye to recognize and savor its subtle beauty. Designed to be viewed rather than strolled in, this small hill-and-pond garden with a court area encourages contemplation from viewing points indoors and from just outside the house. In the entry-way and throughout both wings of the house, glass walls and sliding glass doors link the house and garden.

When they first saw the property, the owners felt a need for enclosure and privacy. Lawn covered the present garden area, and the narrow rear lawn off the small courtyard lay open to a field beyond the property line and to the garden next door. A few handsome trees grew beyond the southwest corner of the lawn, on neighbors' property, but their high trunks provided little screening.

*Viewed from the highest point on a pathway in its southwestern corner, this backyard garden stretches across the width of the property. Out of sight to the far left is the courtyard area.*

## ENCLOSURE AND SITE CHANGES

Need for enclosure and privacy led the homeowners to build a solid fence around the outer garden area and to plant a hedge on the inside of the fence. Eventually the hedge became high enough and thick enough to hide the fence and strike a balance between openness and enclosure.

The lawn that preceded the garden was essentially flat, with a gentle upward slope toward its west end. To enlarge and enliven the flat, small space occupied by lawn, the new design called for variety, richness of detail, and the illusion of depth. In the main area of the garden, beyond the living and dining rooms, a sweep of apparently natural landscape has replaced the lawn. Earth has been built up toward the southwest corner. A narrow mountain stream cascades from the high, forested ground there and slows as it widens into a pool curving around, then disappearing into dense vegetation. In the pond and stream area, a fine assemblage of ancient, lichen-covered stones adds a solid but understated element to the landscape.

Just in front of the flagstone veranda outside the living room, a prayer stone marks the main viewing point, though much the same view may be had from the veranda and the living room. Other important viewing points, each revealing a different scene, are the entryway to the house and the dining room. The main line of sight moves diagonally through the narrow westward side of the garden area and up the stream toward the waterfall and the suggested hilly, forested terrain beyond. An area which was originally of little interest and which posed no challenge to the imagination has been transformed into an evocative Japanese landscape.

## THE ILLUSION OF EXPANSIVENESS

Not only does the topography of this landscape look natural but it also conveys a skillfully contrived illusion of expansiveness, with its long diagonal sight line and the enclosing hedge and plantings that obscure the middle ground between the garden and its surroundings. Borrowed scenery adds to the sense of expansiveness.

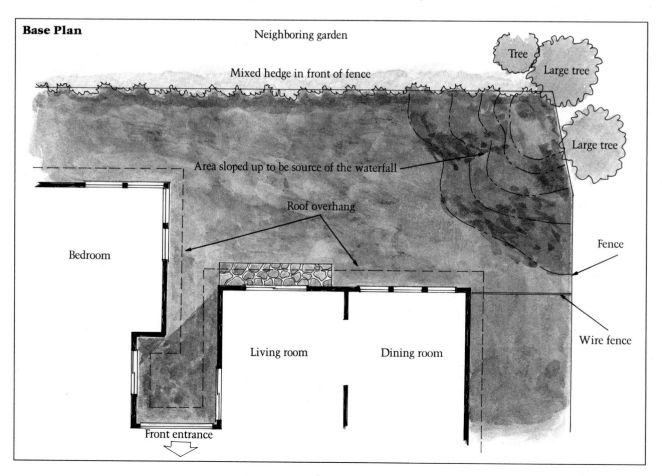

**Base Plan**

Neighboring garden

Mixed hedge in front of fence

Tree

Large tree

Large tree

Area sloped up to be source of the waterfall

Roof overhang

Fence

Bedroom

Wire fence

Living room          Dining room

Front entrance

*The glass walls and simple interior lines make garden and house appear more closely connected. The living-room color scheme is picked up by foliage colors in the garden through nearly nine months of the year. Prominent in the garden are Japanese maples 'Bonfire' and 'Dissectum.'*

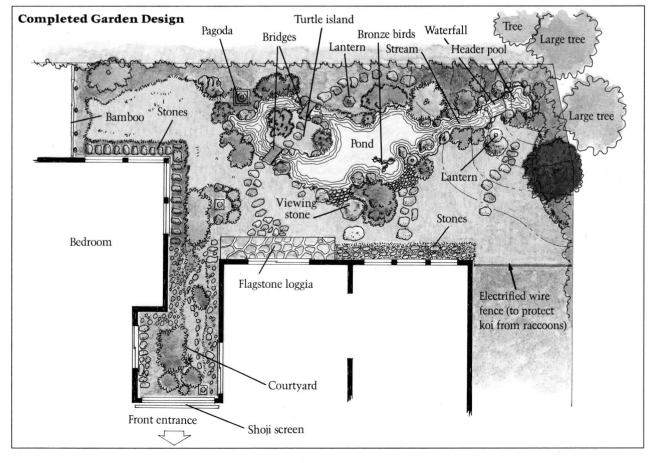

**Completed Garden Design**

Pagoda

Turtle island

Bridges

Lantern

Bronze birds

Stream

Waterfall

Tree

Large tree

Header pool

Bamboo

Stones

Large tree

Pond

Lantern

Viewing stone

Stones

Bedroom

Flagstone loggia

Electrified wire fence (to protect koi from raccoons)

Courtyard

Front entrance

Shoji screen

Especially remarkable in this garden is the fact that the enclosing hedge contributes so strongly to the illusion of depth in a space that is actually shallow. Unlike most occidental hedges, which are characterized by the uniformity given by the use of a single species, such as privet, the hedge in this garden is composed of several species, randomly interplanted to create a tapestry of varying color and texture that gives the illusion of great depth. Looking at the hedge, you might imagine yourself peering into a forest or thicket.

The plantings between the pond and the hedge work visually with the hedge to confuse the viewer's sense of depth and to suggest spaciousness. These shrubs and small trees both obscure the surface of the area between water and hedge and combine with the tall hedge to heighten the effect of a three-dimensional woodland. The textures range from the fineness of pine needles to the boldness of magnolia and rhododendron leaves. Foliage tones range from the muted burgundy leaves of a maple tree to a spectrum of greens bracketed by the brightness of a magnolia and the dusky silveriness of an elaeagnus.

*Above: Standing close to the glass wall of the living room or just outside, on or beyond the veranda, a viewer can look upstream along the main line of sight.*
*Right: The wooded hill and magnificent borrowed scenery beyond—the background trees— create the illusion of a landscape that stretches farther than the garden's actual boundary. In the foreground an old stone pagoda is especially attractive because of its patina of moss and lichen.*

*Right: Seen from just inside the courtyard area, the main part of the garden—with a planted middle ground against the hedge—seems spacious. The corner of the west wing of the house is covered in weathered bamboo, so that architecture and garden are even more related. Note how rectangular stones create a transition between veranda and walkway.*

*Below: A middle ground of shrubs, mossy stones, and the Japanese cutleaf maple against the dark hedge make the shallow rear garden appear deep. A variety of foliage texture and tone adds to the tapestry effect.*

Beyond the upper waterfall and nearly concealed behind the plantings upstream, the dark vine-clad fence helps to erase a garden boundary. The borrowed scenery of the neighbors' large trees becomes part of the impression of a forested hill country from which the stream appears to originate.

Similarly, in the southeast corner of the garden, bamboo is used to great effect to create the illusion that the garden continues outward and around the corner of the house. In reality a fence encloses this tight corner, but the feathery bamboo disguises the fence and implies openness.

## FURTHER USES OF PLANTS

Sensitive plant use in this garden extends beyond creating the illusion of spaciousness. Container plants add variety and, in two instances, dramatic beauty. The owners' experiments with ground covers has also created pleasing results in a mixture of colors and textures throughout the garden. Besides design principles used to suggest expansiveness, other design principles contribute to the effectiveness of this garden's plantings.

*Above: The main sighting line crosses the rear garden diagonally. Notice the contrast between the finely cut leaves of the colored Japanese cutleaf maple in the foreground and the green-leaved species behind it. Baby's tears has made a lush ground cover near the stream and pool.*
*Left: A close look at the ground cover of the garden reveals several plants, though in this section jewel mint of Corsica predominates. The old lantern is surrounded by low junipers, lilyturf, and a carefully shaped Japanese maple.*

Having admired the famous twelfth-century Moss Temple garden of Saiho-ji in Kyoto, where several kinds of mosses have carpeted the ground, the owners were particularly interested in achieving a similar effect. The climate was too dry for true mosses, so they decided to try Irish moss, Scotch moss, blue star creeper, and jewel mint of Corsica. Baby's tears, probably seeded from a neighboring garden, found its way into the experiment. In some areas of the garden, one or more of the mosslike plants adapted; others disappeared. Baby's tears covers much of the pond and stream area. Around the layered pine near the west side of the garden, blue star creeper has won out. In some places, several ground covers coexist happily, creating a brocade of greens; a sprinkling of tiny blossoms adorns each species in its season.

Unity and simplicity, rather than clutter and crowding, characterize the plantings of the garden—largely because of the owners' skillful employment of two design principles: repetition and simplification. Only two varieties of juniper are used; their use is widespread, and their prevalence contributes a sense of cohesiveness. Other plants have been similarly repeated.

## SPECIAL AND FINISHING TOUCHES

Close to the rear of the house, a practical need led to a charming motif for the garden. Poor drainage and, in the rainy season, resulting soggy soil required that the area beneath the living and dining room eaves be dug and filled with drainage pipe and stones. The owners took advantage of this necessity by covering under-eave areas with cobbles to give the impression of the traditional Japanese drainage troughs that catch water from roofs. On top of the cobbles they placed a few larger stones, round ones in some areas, roughly rectilinear ones elsewhere. The troughs eliminate the need for planting these sometimes very dry and dark areas, and they create a pleasing transition from the strict geometry of the house to the freer forms of the garden.

Other transitional devices evolved over several years. Instead of letting asymmetric stepping stones begin abruptly at the rectangular flagstone veranda, the owners decided

*The cobbled surface under the eaves of the courtyard area provides a graceful link between the house and the garden. Shoji not only serve the practical functions of framing and regulating the view but also add, both outdoors and indoors, to the Japanese atmosphere.*

*Above: Shoji screens in the entryway fold back to reveal the courtyard area of the garden. Prominent here is the ancient Hinoki cypress.*
*Opposite above: The cluster of stones offers a visual transition from veranda to garden but also makes it easier for a viewer to avoid wet ground.*
*Opposite below: The short, natural-looking, stone-slab bridge is anchored by stones in the traditional manner. The juniper to the upper right is* Juniperus horizontalis *'Variegata'.*

to use a cluster of stepping stones to start each of two small stepping-stone paths. One cluster consists of more or less rectangular stones that link the veranda with the irregular forms of the stones along the path. Similarly, the careful shaping of the Japanese maple in the courtyard gives, from certain angles, a subtly squared-off form whose sides align with the surrounding sides of the house—another transition between the symmetry of the house and the asymmetry of the garden.

A bold touch provides a transition not so much from symmetry to asymmetry as from the polished formality of the interior to the rusticity of the garden. From the entryway a section of exterior wall is visible in the garden. To blend the wood siding of the house with the garden, the owners added a screen of woven bamboo, suggestive of a Japanese garden fence.

To frame the view of the garden in the Japanese manner, the owners used shoji (folding rice-paper screens) on the glass wall looking out from the entryway. Shoji offer the advantage of controlling the view: The whole garden vista, or only a portion, may be revealed by the folding screens.

It wasn't long after building the pond and filling it with carp that the owners realized the menace posed to the fish by raccoons. So they installed an unobtrusive metal grille just below the surface of a section of the pond. The carp retreat underneath it when threatened and, for much of the year, lily pads obscure it. It's a simple matter to control mosquito larvae in the pond: Remember that overfed fish ignore larvae, but hungry fish eat them.

At some point in this garden's evolution, its creators found a worthy use for a prized porcelain jardiniere. Now inverted and nestled near the water's edge, it furnishes the perfect spot to sit and contemplate the garden.

## Mail-Order Sources

It's always better to buy from a local nursery, where you can inspect your purchase and don't have to pay shipping charges. But if you can't locate the plants or materials you want locally, these mail-order sources specialize in plants and features described in the text.

**Bonsai Farm**
Box 130
Lavernia, TX 78121
*Bonsai plants, tools, pots, books*

**The Cummins Garden**
22 Robertsville Road
Marlboro, NJ 07746
201-536-2591
*Dwarf rhododendrons, azaleas, dwarf conifers*

**Endangered Species**
Box 1830
Tustin, CA 92680
714-544-9505
*Bamboos*

**Kurt Bluemel, Inc.**
2740 Greene Lane
Baldwin, MD 21013
301-557-7229
*Bamboos, ferns, perennials*

**Lilypons Water Gardens**
Box 10
Lilypons, MD 21717-0010
301-874-5133
*Ponds and water plants*

**Matsu-Momiji Nursery**
Box 11414
Philadelphia, PA 19111
215-722-6286
*Japanese maples and pines*

**Nampara Gardens**
2004 Golf Course Road
Bayside, CA 95524
707-822-5744
*Redwood lanterns and bridges*

**Paradise Water Gardens**
14 May Street
Whitman, MA 02382
617-447-4711
*Water plants*

**Philip Hawk & Company**
159 East College Avenue
Pleasant Gap, PA 16823
814-355-7177
*Stone lanterns*

**Robert Bruce of Berkeley**
2910 Telegraph Avenue
Berkeley, CA 94705
415-845-7424
*Stone lanterns*

**Shanti Bithi Nursery**
3047 High Ridge Road
Stamford, CT 06903
203-329-0768
*Bonsai plants, tools, and pots; stone lanterns*

**Slocum Water Gardens**
Dept. H-37
1101 Cypress Gardens Road
Winter Haven, FL 33880
*Water plants, pools, fish*

**Smith & Hawken**
25 Corte Madera
Mill Valley, CA 94941
415-383-4050
*Japanese pruning tools*

**Van Ness Water Gardens**
2460 North Euclid Avenue
Upland, CA 91786-1199
714-982-2425
*Water plants, pond-construction materials, pumps, pond supplies*

**Washington Evergreen Nursery**
Box 388AH
Leicester, NC 23748
704-683-4518
*Dwarf conifers*

**Waterford Gardens**
74 East Allendale Road
Saddle River, NJ 07458
201-327-0721
*Water plants, pools and accessories, fish*

## Books for Further Reading

Bring, Mitchell and Wayembergh, Josse. *Design and Meaning in Japanese Gardens.* New York: McGraw Hill, 1981.

Brooklyn Botanical Gardens. *Japanese Gardens—Plants and Gardens, Brooklyn Botanic Garden Record Series.* New York: Brooklyn Botanical Gardens, 1985.

Hayakawa, Matsao. *The Garden Art of Japan.* New York and Tokyo: Weatherhill/Heibosha, 1973.

Itho, Teiji and Sosei, Kuzunishi. *Space and Illusion in the Japanese Garden.* New York: Weatherhill, 1980.

Kuck, Loraine. *The World of the Japanese Garden: From Chinese Origins to Modern Landscape Art.* New York and Tokyo: Weatherhill, 1968.

Seike, Kiyoshi; Masanobu, Kudo; and Engel, David H. *A Japanese Touch for Your Garden.* New York and Tokyo: Kodansha International, 1980.

Shigemori, Kanto. *The Japanese Courtyard Garden: Landscapes for Small Spaces.* New York and Tokyo: Weatherhill, 1981.

Yoshimura, Yuji and Halford, M. Giovanna. *The Japanese Art of Miniature Trees and Landscapes: Their Creation, Care, and Enjoyment.* Rutland, Vt. and Tokyo: Tuttle, 1957.

# Climate Zone Map

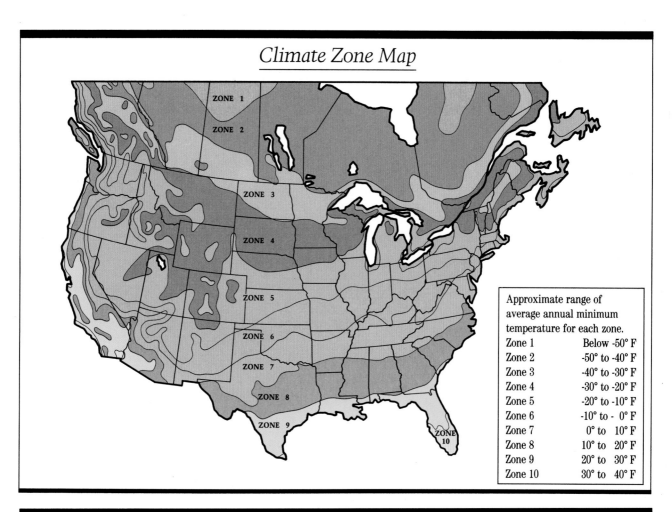

Approximate range of average annual minimum temperature for each zone.

|  | |
|---|---|
| Zone 1 | Below -50° F |
| Zone 2 | -50° to -40° F |
| Zone 3 | -40° to -30° F |
| Zone 4 | -30° to -20° F |
| Zone 5 | -20° to -10° F |
| Zone 6 | -10° to - 0° F |
| Zone 7 | 0° to 10° F |
| Zone 8 | 10° to 20° F |
| Zone 9 | 20° to 30° F |
| Zone 10 | 30° to 40° F |

# U.S. Measure and Metric Measure Conversion Chart

| | Symbol | Formulas for Exact Measures | | | Rounded Measures for Quick Reference | | |
|---|---|---|---|---|---|---|---|
| | | When you know: | Multiply by: | To find: | | | |
| **Mass** | oz | ounces | 28.35 | grams | 1 oz | | = 30 g |
| **(Weight)** | lb | pounds | 0.45 | kilograms | 4 oz | | = 115 g |
| | g | grams | 0.035 | ounces | 8 oz | | = 225 g |
| | kg | kilograms | 2.2 | pounds | 16 oz | = 1 lb | = 450 g |
| | | | | | 32 oz | = 2 lb | = 900 g |
| | | | | | 36 oz | = 2¼ lb | = 1000g (1 kg) |
| **Volume** | pt | pints | 0.47 | liters | 1 c | = 8 oz | = 250 ml |
| | qt | quarts | 0.95 | liters | 2 c (1 pt) | = 16 oz | = 500 ml |
| | gal | gallons | 3.785 | liters | 4 c (1 qt) | = 32 oz | = 1 liter |
| | ml | milliliters | 0.034 | fluid ounces | 4 qt (1 gal) | = 128 oz | = 3¾ liter |
| **Length** | in. | inches | 2.54 | centimeters | ⅜ in. | = 1 cm | |
| | ft | feet | 30.48 | centimeters | 1 in. | = 2.5 cm | |
| | yd | yards | 0.9144 | meters | 2 in. | = 5 cm | |
| | mi | miles | 1.609 | kilometers | 2½ in. | = 6.5 cm | |
| | km | kilometers | 0.621 | miles | 12 in. (1 ft) | = 30 cm | |
| | m | meters | 1.094 | yards | 1 yd | = 90 cm | |
| | cm | centimeters | 0.39 | inches | 100 ft | = 30 m | |
| | | | | | 1 mi | = 1.6 km | |
| **Temperature** | °F | Fahrenheit | ⅝ (after subtracting 32) | Celsius | 32°F | = 0°C | |
| | °C | Celsius | ⅝ (then add 32) | Fahrenheit | 212°F | = 100°C | |
| **Area** | in.² | square inches | 6.452 | square centimeters | 1 in.² | = 6.5 cm² | |
| | ft² | square feet | 929.0 | square centimeters | 1 ft² | = 930 cm² | |
| | yd² | square yards | 8361.0 | square centimeters | 1 yd² | = 8360 cm² | |
| | a. | acres | 0.4047 | hectares | 1 a. | = 4050 m² | |